CONFESSIONS OF THE
ACCUSED

Paperback ISBN 978-1-961874-00-8
Hardcover ISBN 978-1-961874-00-5
E-Book ISBN 978-1-961874-02-2
Audio Book ISBN 978-1-961874-03-9

www.onemoorepage.com
email: info@onemoorepage.com

CONFESSIONS OF THE
ACCUSED

THE SHOCKING TRUE STORY
OF A SIXTEEN-YEAR-OLD SENTENCED TO LIFE

DERREL MOORE JR.

CONFESSIONS OF THE ACCUSED

DEDICATION

I dedicate this book to my daughter, De'aira and her two little girls. I pray through my story you will find your own, and that it will inspire you to be the best you. Your father loves you, please forgive me, and know that I left me long before I left you.

CONTENTS

DERREL MOORE JR.

ACKNOWLEDGEMENTS

My sincere thanks to God, it is you alone that I praise and you alone that I owe for my existence. Thank you for all of it. To those that helped me in life regardless of individual motives or the outcome of those relationships, I thank God for having inspired you, and I thank each of you for those efforts. I know I'm not the easiest person to love and you know that I shy away from accepting help from others but somehow you helped me and loved me anyway.

Thank you, thank you, THANK YOU. Angie, I highlight you because you've been everything I needed exactly when I needed it. You remained a true friend despite the noise. Thanks my Rose, heaven has a place just for you. Nicole, you made me a father, I'll be forever grateful for that alone, but since then you've become a friend, and I cherish that just as much.

To the extended Austin and Moore family, I will forever be grateful to those who loved me through my process despite my failures. Dina, you've been a friend when a friend was needed most, thanks and a special shout out to ATL. Since the original writing of this book a few major events have taken place; some sad, one of which was the untimely and senseless murder of my brother and friend, Shamel Parker. May your soul rest my brother, I love you.

Ma Duke and Granny, thanks for showing me love; we're family forever. Jennifer, "If not for you..." is all I need to say, thank you lady. Jassy, God sent you for a reason and a season. Thanks for being his servant and for being a friend. I cherish it and regret the short comings. So many have come into my life for just a second or a minute to help me get through the moments in time when I was in my darkest hours. You know who you are and you can trust I'll never forget. It helped in ways you will never truly know. Thank you!

Dad, I can only try to imagine the pain you've experienced because of the decisions I've made in my life. Thanks for never giving up on me and for always loving me even as I made mistakes and struggled to get it right. You never failed to let me know you love me. Thanks Pops.

Granny Love and my grandfather, may you both find peace and rest in it. The two of you showed me what real love looks like. My dearest Granny Love, I'm going to do my best to pay all my debts that I owe in this life so one day we can meet again. I love you my lady. Mom, it would take a book to list my many thanks, so I'm writing it. You were just a girl when you found out you were pregnant with me. With all your dreams of becoming a pop-star and a host of possibilities ahead of you, you chose me instead. You loved me like no other. Your love for me was so selfish you refused to have more children, always telling me all your love was for me and you had no more left to give. I love how you did your best with the tools you had to raise me. Please know that it was because of you, by God's permission that I survived and eventually figured out my reason why. I love you Doll.

A special thanks to my uncles Robert, Ricky, and Mike, I learned valuable lessons from all of you. My cousin Ebony (aka pretty eyes), you know I love you. You're more than just a cousin; you're my big sister. I love you and the kids with all my heart. Mae, I love you like cooked food. Chantilly, please know I love you and your kids, I root for you in life. Aunt Wanda, you are my girl. I miss you and love you. You taught me the game, now no one can beat me in spades, not even you, "the master" LOL. Monique, Shawn, Nicole, Snapper, Nakia, and Gina, family matters, I forgive all of you, I love you more than you know. Monet, I want you to know that I understand. To all that I've caused harm of any kind, please forgive me. Now that I know better, I promise I'll do better. As for those who hurt me in any way, I forgive you and thank you for the lessons of growth. I learned from you.

Last but certainly not least, after so much turmoil and loss, God has provided me with you. I could not have asked for a better life partner. You are my teammate, my everything, and meeting you, loving you and being loved by you has made all the struggle worth it. Before meeting you I was already amazed by God's love for me, and now coupled with that awe, I am stuck in a state of gratitude and happiness because I worship and serve a God as merciful as the one that created you, and allowed me to be loved by you. Thank you Nicci (my Queen Buttercup) for loving me despite our differences. I will live my life being thankful to God for you and I will show it by being faithful and dutiful to you and to our union. I LOVE You!

INTRODUCTION

For many years I've warred with myself on the direction of this book. My goal is to serve not only the youth who are foolishly chasing down my fate, but also to provide parents, community leaders and the judicial system with a meaningful glimpse into the realities of the impoverished, misunderstood, and troubled youth of our nation (especially young Black men). The motivations of these young men are similar to those of the school shooter who is so desperate to draw attention to his plight and his grievances that he is willing to die in an irrational and insane fashion; not in hopes of heaven or justification, but in hopes that someone will notice. In hopes that someone will care enough to inquire, "what condition would cause this person to choose such a senseless and dead-end road?" or "What can be done to address these cancerous conditions so that no one else will ever feel so hopeless that they would intentionally choose to tread such a treacherous path?"

Well, I was one of the hopeless. This book is my attempt to answer those questions with my selfless and vulnerable truth, offered in a manner that people like me who come from the bottom can relate to. So, as I sit here held captive in a corner of the world that most don't even know exists, this is my only outlet to rise above the outcome of my actions and be accountable. This is my truth. At first, I planned to write it as fiction and change all the names, places, and dates, but that would only allow the lies to live.

I cannot lay here wallowing in misery and thoughts of what might have been. I must move forward. This book is a cry...no, a roar. I want you to hear us, and try to understand us, the ones who are so often lost, left, let down and forgotten. And if you dare to judge, I ask that you also dare to save, because despite our disfunction, we are also created by God, in his image. We are worth saving. We are more valuable than most of you know. Personally, I had to lose everything before I found the strength to save myself. Yet I still sit here, held captive with so much to offer, and so many memories of how I got here.

To those of you who are living a lifestyle that will land you where I am, please read my story; feel and feed off my pain. Understand that you must take steps to save yourself, because for most people like us, there is no savior in the system. There is typically no understanding. You will be judged, condemned, and persecuted; in the streets, you may be killed. So, if you can, I beg you to be strong enough not to live my life, but learn from it. See the mistakes I made and run from them. Trust me when I tell you a life in the streets is filled with loss, hatred, jealousy, death, and a great deal of regret.

To be clear, this book is not an excuse for my past behavior. I take full responsibility for the actions and the folly of my youth. I apologize for what those horrible choices cost other people. I pray that anyone I've ever hurt or caused any pain can one day find peace and forgive me for my actions. Unfortunately (as well as fortunately), we learn as we live, and as I have grown to know better, I have done better. I cannot take back my yesterdays or the mistakes I made in them, I can only do better today, now that I know better. All I can hope for is that the people who read this book or encounter my work through my community outreach projects will take a look at my experiences in the inner city or "the ghetto" and make an effort to better understand the reality of the impoverished and troubled youth, especially our most vulnerable black boys.

We are crying out for help when we resort to trading in our schoolbooks and athletic dreams for drugs and guns. We want the American dream as much as anyone else (and we deserve it) but we've only experienced the American nightmare. In order to survive, as the resilient and adaptable human beings that we are, we adjust to this grim reality pretty quickly. We become masters of the monstrous conditions we encounter. So, just as we took the despicable word "nigger" and turned it into a somewhat socially acceptable term of endearment, we have transformed hunting and killing each other into a blood-sport. This is not a coincidence. We feel worthless, so we act accordingly. We were born into this. We did not ask for this hate. We inherited this evil.

The multitudes of men and women in positions of power and influence seem to engage in one of two courses of action. They either fumble around with programs and policies that seldom (if ever) bear fruit, or they wait on the sidelines for us to rescue ourselves. I'm not sure this is practical, but I'm certain it's not justice. Sadly, most have somehow been convinced that there is no hope for us. The majority has decided to take this falsehood to heart. They've chosen to ignore, avoid, overlook, and neglect us. Ultimately, most in society have abandoned us to our own emotional and immature devices, leaving us to destroy one another for reasons we don't even understand at ages as young as fourteen and fifteen years old.

I ask that those of you that are in a position of affluence and/or influence take a step back and reassess our situation. Get to know us and our lived experience before you judge us. And then if you dare to judge, be daring enough to help save. I ask that you roll up your sleeves, get your hands dirty and help save the next troubled child you see. Don't be the person full of opinions but failing to offer any solutions. Do not be the one that sits high and looks low without having a clue.

This book is not just my story. This is not just my problem. It is our collective human story, and our problem to confront together. It would be shortsighted for us to pretend it doesn't exist. We can continue to watch kids like me go to prison with life sentences for crimes they can't even spell (let alone conceive of their consequences) or we can address the underlying causes of juvenile crime and violence, and do something about them.

The truth contained here will hurt some feelings (it hurts mine). Some family secrets will be exposed; it will not be pretty. My father will feel betrayed, and he does not deserve it. As I reveal this raw truth, it is very humbling because more than anything, it will remove my own mask, and my own facades will be destroyed. My entire family will never look at me the same. My daughter will know things I never wanted her to. This is not easy. It is very scary, and I don't want to do it. However, I am convicted by the Spirit of God that it is necessary. I cannot know better and ignore my obligations to do better. I cannot keep my testimony to myself. I cannot hide my light under a bushel. So here it is. Read my truth, just remember, if you dare to judge...

DERREL MOORE JR.

CHAPTER ONE
Lessons Children Shouldn't Learn

At five years old I had the best a child could have, two loving parents together and in love. I was in school and had lots of friends. I remember distinctly wanting to be a fireman when I grew up. I wanted to be a hero. I wanted to save people from burning homes and buildings. No one could tell me I would not grow up to be a hero just like Superman. I would never have imagined my life as it is. My mother, Darlene Austin, was a well-built beautiful Black woman. She had the kind of curves men die for. Her skin was caramel brown, and she stood no more than five feet tall. She had gorgeous almond shaped brown eyes and a singing voice that would remind you of Whitney Houston. Just a few short notes and you'd want to hear her sing all day long. Growing up she used to tell me she chose me over her own dreams of becoming a superstar, and I am not alone when I tell you she could easily have made it.

1

My father, Derrel Moore Sr., was her exact opposite. Where she was short, and petite, he is tall and huge. He's a classic man's man, the kind of guy women fall for at first sight. He has the brightest smile and can charm a woman in sixty seconds flat, a trait that often got him in trouble. Tall, dark, and handsome with a slick tongue to match. There is no doubt he loved my mother. They were childhood sweethearts, and the world was theirs to conquer.

One warm summer day as I dreamed the innocent dreams that five-year-old boys dream, I was awakened by my mother screaming. I was disoriented and had no idea what was going on, but I knew my mom was being hurt. In my mind I was a hero, so I ran to her screams with sleep in my eyes and no fear in my heart. I was going to protect my mother at all costs; that's what heroes do (especially for their own mom).

When I burst into her bedroom door, I saw something I've never been able to shake. My mother was on the bed crying out in pain while being hit. Instead of some monster or strange man swinging, it was my own father, my hero. He was beating my mother. When I screamed, "Get off my mommy!" he froze. The look on my mother's face still haunts me. When she saw me witness such inexcusable violence from the man responsible for showing me how to be a man, it broke her bone deep. I could see it in her eyes. In that moment, I began to change. My fantasy life took a blow that day that I'm still recovering from. I love my parents, but at that moment my little confused heart was forced to choose.

On my mother's face was pain, love, regret, and deep remorse for the position they had put me in. I could see that she was distraught about her child, her baby, seeing her this way. My father's face was filled with rage, anger, and denial; traits that would soon become my own armor and my closest companions. My father commanded me to, "Get Out!" In that moment I became acquainted with another trait that would later become one of the sharpest tools in my box, defiance.

The hero in me jumped on his back. It didn't matter that he was well over six feet tall and built like an oak, while I was all of three feet, slender, built like a sapling. I was on his back screaming, kicking, and pulling at him. "Get off my mommy!" I screamed, but he was too far gone. He rose up from the position where he was bent over my mother. I was forced to stop swinging my tiny fists and try to hang on. To a five-year-old he was a giant. He tossed me off his back. The fall was long, scary, and violent. He started in on my mother again but when he saw that I was getting up and approaching to engage in round two, something came over him and he just left the house in a rage.

When we were done crying, consoling each other,

and mourning our respective losses, my mom got me dressed. She got herself together and then we walked hand in hand down Jefferson Avenue in Buffalo, New York to Landon Street. We went to a place where we always found sanctuary when times got tough, Granny's house. This was a home where even a stranger could go in and find peace. A place where one could find refuge, a kind word, and a great meal. It was here where wounds got licked and hearts got healed. It's the love I got and learned from my grandparents in that place that I cling to now. Their example and demonstration of love is what I've called on from time to time to find my way back from a life of pain. I've called on that love for the strength to open up and tell my truth.

When we finally made it to my grandparents' house we came in with all smiles and some story my mom fabricated and made me go along with to keep things calm. We would later learn that my Granny Love, my mother's mom, was no fool. She knew something was wrong. She always knew, but her house was the place people ran to for love, not judgment. My grandmother, Sylvia Beatrice Austin, was small in stature like my mom. She was just the heavyset version. She had the heart of a lioness. She would fight for all that she loved; and my grandmother loved everyone. My grandmother, despite her knocks in life, had a peace about her that was admirable. She had so many past experiences that she could have used as an excuse to be bitter, but her faith in God refused to allow her to let life knock her down without getting right back up. My grandfather, James "Bootsie" Drakeford, was not my mother's biological father, but he was truly the only fully formed example I had growing up of what a man is.

He met my grandmother after she'd had several bad relationships and experiences with men. When they met, she already had four children by different men. My uncle Mike was a newborn. My mother was a toddler, and my grandfather treated her as the beautiful little princess that she was. This was back in the nineteen sixties, when an unwed mother was an outcast, but he treated my Granny Love as a Queen.

My grandfather was dark as night in complexion. He stood about five feet eight inches tall, but his character was that of a giant. He loved my grandmother's four children and the baby girl they had together all the same. They were a family; nowhere near perfect, but a family indeed. As this day started with violence and confusion, my mother did the best she could to make me forget the traumatizing event that we had experienced. We didn't talk about it at all, we pretended it didn't happen. She fed me my favorite foods and I was allowed to go play with my friends. Most of my friends lived on Landon Street. For me this was home. Our address was a few blocks away, but my heart lived there on Landon Street. I ran up and down and played until night stole the day. The beauty of the mind of a child (its malleability), is one of God's many gifts. This youthful quality is what allowed me to forget about the earlier trouble and carry on with just being a kid.

My mother had the most beautiful voice I've ever heard; it was also the loudest. When she was looking for me, let's just say the entire neighborhood knew about it. "Bootie!!! Bootie!!!" That was my mother calling for me in the neighborhood. Bootie was her pet name for me and it got me ruthlessly teased by my friends. Everyone knows kids can be cruel without even realizing it, and my friends were no different. That nickname led to a lot of rumbles. I always had to fight for my respect.

That day, after hearing my mother's dreaded screams of "Bootie" buzzing through the air on Landon Street, I came into the house, got washed up and ate more of my favorite foods. Back then I could eat macaroni and cheese with pork chops every single day. There was no one that could make macaroni and cheese like my mom. Don't get me wrong, my Granny Love was the best cook ever, but my mother's macaroni...forget about it, simply the best! After eating I was too tired to even realize I was no longer at my mom and dad's house in my own bed that was huge and fit for a prince. I was at my Granny's house;

in my heart of hearts this was home.

I was sleeping like a baby, only to be awakened once again to the sound of disturbing noise. This time it was many voices, and violent sounds. I heard my mom, my dad, my uncle, my grandparents and my aunt Wanda. The hero in me was once again activated. I ran to my mother's aid, and saw my mother, my grandparents, and my aunt Wanda trying to pull at my uncle Robert. He was fighting my father, violently hitting him. With each blow he roared, "Keep your hands off my sister!" My mother was crying, begging him to stop. She professed her love for my father and pleaded with my uncle to leave my father alone.

My uncle looked at her like she was crazy and left in what can only be described as disgusted rage. My mother turned to try to console my father, but he spurned her affection believing that she had broken their bond and trust. He left the house upset, as if he was the one who had been victimized earlier that morning. My mom cried and I did my best to calm her as she held me tight. It was hard. I was five years old. My life was perfect yesterday but now I was afraid that every time I went to sleep something bad would happen.

As I write this I now realize why to this very day, many years later, I still struggle with sleep. I fight it off, and then when I need it, I'm forced to fight for it. Since that summer when I was five years old to this very day, no matter what, sleep has been my enemy, in that it has been so elusive. After a few days, my mom and dad made up. The two of them never asked for my opinion, after all I was just a kid; and in truth, at that time I most likely would not have had the ability to express my feelings. I was scared. My father had become a monster to me. Where it was once easy to talk to him, I was now reserved. I had to watch what I said, and mostly I said nothing. My mother only needed a few days, maybe dinner, and whatever promises he had made. I don't know. What I do know is, I needed him to give back the security and safety his actions had stolen from me. I needed my father back.

Instead, I got a dog. And still to this day we've never had that needed talk, which explains why our bond, although alive, is still strained to a degree. My dad got me a dog and I fell instantly in love with him. He was all I had to talk to when I was at my mom and dad's house. My mother and father were in love, and young love knows no bounds. They loved me, but neither really knew or understood what I needed. I would talk to my dog. I told him everything I was afraid to say to them. I was scared. I didn't look at my father the same, and I could not sleep. I barely ate. I was confused and lived in fear that my dad would hurt us again. I say us, because you don't get to hurt a child's mother without simultaneously hurting that child.

My parents kept asking me to name my dog, but I couldn't think of one. I was in a state of depression at the age of five. My mom would ask me what was wrong, and my go-to response was, "nothing". Inside I was screaming, "everything!"

I would beg to go home. My mom would say, "You are at home." So, I would say, "I want to go to my Granny house." My mom tried to break me out of it, but my home was where my heart was, and that was 85 Landon Street. I will never forget this day; it was close to school time. I was kind of nervous but also excited. All my friends were at school #53. I could not wait to see them because I didn't get to see them much. After the fight between my dad and my uncle, my dad didn't want us over there as much. But, on this particular day, he dropped us off because he had things to do. So, I went to see my Granny Love (that's what I call her.) I gave her the biggest hug, and immediately I was out of my shell. I don't know if my mom noticed, but I would blossom when my father was not around. I went outside to play with my friends. I told them about my cool new dog, and promised I would bring him next time. I still hadn't given him a name, so my friends and I started thinking of names. I was thinking Dino, just like Fred Flintstone's pet.

I had a lot of fun that day. Then I heard my mom calling me with that infamous and embarrassing nickname loud as ever, Bootie!!! I would try to ignore her. I could not stand that name. My friends would tease me and say, your mother is calling you Bootie. We would end up rolling in the dirt, play fighting because they called me Bootie. I just didn't like anyone but her calling me that. My aunt Wanda would call me that and even my mom's friend Yolanda. There were a select few that would call me that, but as I got older, I would only answer one person calling me Bootie. I think my mother, who lasted the longest calling me Bootie, had come up with that name because when she had me, she finally got a bootie (as the story goes).

I finally stopped rolling in the dirt in back of 77 Landon Street with my friends over them teasing me about that nickname. My mother's voice was getting louder and closer, so I tried to dust myself off as I ran out front. I answered her with a smile on my face, trying to hide my mischievous behavior. When I got out there, I noticed my father's car, a red and white Boxer. My smile vanished as I realized he was back, and we were leaving. I begged to stay to no avail. I went back to the house to say my goodbyes to Granny Love. My grandfather, who I called Bootsie like everyone else, was at work. He worked day and night to take care of his family. After saying my goodbyes, I reluctantly approached the car with my mother and father inside. I hopped in the backseat. My father greeted me, and I returned his greeting, but it was obvious to everyone in the car I was not enthused. To them I was likely just upset about leaving my friends (and maybe that was a part of it) but the part they didn't seem to understand is that more than just being upset, I was scared.

He pulled off down Landon and I waved goodbye to my friends. I knew I probably wouldn't see them again until school started even though we only lived around the corner on Jefferson Avenue. When we got to the house and pulled in the driveway, I was looking forward to seeing my dog. I finally had a name in mind for him. It had been a few weeks and it was time to give him a name. I didn't see him on his chain in the backyard. He was just a puppy, and because he wasn't house broken yet, my dad put him outside whenever we left. I looked and looked, but I could not find my dog. My dad looked around too... nothing.

I was inconsolable. I cried and cried about my dog. My mother didn't really like animals, but she felt my pain, so she asked my father to go find my dog. My dad went back out to talk to some neighbors and when he returned sometime later, he had the dog leash, and a sad look on his face. He didn't know how to tell me what happened to my dog, so he told my mom. The neighbor's dog had gotten loose. He came in our backyard and killed my dog. I was devastated. I did not understand why one dog would do this to another dog. I cried like a baby. In this moment, I learned I was living in a dog-eat-dog world.

A few days later after a lot of crying my dad came into the house with a pair of jeans. He told me they were from the neighbor. This man's dog had eaten my dog and he sent me a pair of jeans. My grief turned to anger. This is my first memory of my own rage, but I held it in. I could not trust my father with my feelings. He had become a source of fear. There was no doubt he loved me, but I just couldn't forget that look in his eyes when he was attacking my mother. By this time school was in session and I went with a chip on my shoulders. I was only five, but I was old for my age. I went to school knowing that fathers beat mothers, dogs eat dogs, and sometimes your house ain't home.

To make things worse I was afraid to sleep because bad things happened whenever I did. We lived in a large one-bedroom apartment and my bed was in the same room as my parent's. My mom and dad didn't know I was having trouble sleeping. They would send me to bed first and then wait to come in, thinking I would be asleep. They would smoke their weed in the living room, listen to music, then come to bed long after I should have been knocked out. They were young and in love and expressed that love physically. They had no idea, but I was awake, and I saw and heard it all.

I went to school at five, exposed to so many of life's realities. My fantasy no longer existed. I still held on to my dream of being a fireman, but my perfect life was over. I was a kid with issues. I had a huge chip on my shoulder. I had no one to talk to, my dog was dead, and at school #53 there was no outlet for troubled kids. All troubled kids got back then was sent to the principal's office where we would be threatened with a trip to see Mr. Patterson. He was known for using his paddle to reprimand kids that misbehaved. I was defiant. So, I had no fear of this well-known threat. I was beginning to retreat into my shell. I did just enough to be considered a smart student but not enough to really excel. I didn't act out too much that year, so my issues weren't obvious. I was seen as an introvert. Most of my problems that year were in my head, heart, and house.

The fights between my parents continued, but they learned to keep them under wraps, so they didn't directly involve me. At least that's what they told themselves. They argued a lot. My mom accused my father of cheating all the time. We would move in and out. It would be good for a week and then something would happen, and she'd be packing us up to leave. It went on and on back and forth. I became insecure and grew even more distant from my father. I saw my mother cry over and over. I couldn't help her because her pain was coming from my father, and despite the toxic nature of their relationship, she loved him. I felt helpless, and I blamed him. In all of their fighting, and all the noise, I was the casualty of their war. While it's easy to see now, back then when they were young and dumb, they had no idea what their behavior was doing to me.

Around this time my paternal grandmother passed away and it was the worst thing to happen to us. We were already a very fragile, disfunctional family, and losing her destroyed us. My father loved his mother beyond all measure and so did I. She was full of nothing but love. Then she was gone. I felt robbed (still do). All I remember is her love. She truly cared for me and would never allow my father to be less than a man to me. When she passed, a part of me did as well. I remember the day of her funeral. I jumped on her casket as she was being carried from the church and begged to go with her. I don't remember much else but her love, and that I wanted to go too. Something in me knew things were about to get worse, and they did.

CHAPTER TWO
Sex Miseducation At Six

I nevitably, it came to a point where my mother couldn't take it anymore; she couldn't deal with my father anymore. So, once again she abruptly told me we were moving...for good this time. We went back to my grandparents' house, and I was in heaven. I was doing well in school. My mother was always out on the town. When she wasn't out chasing after my father, she was clubbing all night with her friends. The immaturity of youth got the best of her. She was pregnant with me at sixteen. She was just a kid, and my father was all she knew. In truth, up to that point, she hadn't really lived. She'd basically gone straight from high school to housewife (minus the marriage). So, she started acting out and running the streets.

Granny Love would get sick of it. She would load me in her car to go looking for my mother in all of her usual hang out spots. I remember one night in particular, my Granny found her at a bar called "the

133". She went in and dragged my mother out. She told her, "You're a mother. You have a son to raise. You don't get to run the streets all night, every night." My Granny gave her an ear full and put her in the car to take her home. As we were heading home, my mother hopped out the moving car like a stunt woman. She rolled in the street and then jumped up, running away in the opposite direction.

My mom was drunk, and high, but most of all she was hurt. I can only imagine her thoughts. I looked just like my dad, the man she fiercely loved and halfway hated. She couldn't bear it. She was running from so much more than I could understand back then, but in my six-year-old mind, it seemed like she was running from me. This kind of volatile behavior went on for a long time, so Granny Love picked up the pieces and took care of me. She did her best to guide my mother out of the darkness, and she never missed a beat when it came to loving me. Then out of nowhere, my mom forgave my dad and with no notice or warning we were packing our things to move back in with him.

This time we lived on the other side of town. My dad had moved to Delaware Avenue downtown in a predominantly white neighborhood. I was far from my friends, and more distant than ever from my father. I hadn't really seen him much since the last split. It was like when my mom broke up with him, he broke up with me. The figurative distance did more damage than the physical and caused serious harm to our father/son relationship. Men, I implore you, do not allow the relationship (or lack thereof) with the mother of your child (ren) to determine the kind of relationship you have with your offspring. There is simply no excuse that will do, and they will never understand.

By the time we moved back in, my father was openly dealing drugs. I never knew how he earned money before. I had never thought to question his income, but by this time I was developing rapidly and becoming quite precocious. I was being exposed to all kinds of things. So, I wasn't shocked to learn he was dealing weed. He didn't try to hide it. I think my parents believed I was too young to possibly understand. But the fact is that he couldn't hide it even if he wanted to. We lived in a studio apartment, and he literally had a garbage bag twice my size full of weed sitting in the bedroom area of the apartment. I used to play on it like it was a beanbag. They would party and deal drugs right there, lying to themselves about my ability to comprehend. At the very least, they figured I wouldn't remember it later in life. These lies become the sand in which we bury our heads when we don't want to see the consequences of our own recklessness.

The truth is, if a child can see or hear, then that

child has the ability to retain whatever is seen and heard. Having seen and heard way too much myself, I stand as a living testament to what the mind of a child can keep locked away in their memory. For all you parents that are blessed to have little gifts born to you by the direct permission of God, be careful what you present to that gift.

By the time I turned six years old I was seriously struggling with my father issues. Things got a little better when we moved back in, but I still didn't trust him. There was always chaos and confusion between my parents revolving around allegations of my father cheating on my mom. The cycle started all over again. She would pick up and leave at a moment's notice and I'd be dragged along for the ride. We could be gone a day or a month, it all depended on how long it would take for them to work it out. There was one thing that was for sure, my dad did not know how to be a father when they broke up, and to be fair, my mom really didn't know how to let him be one.

Whenever he would try to see me while they were broken up, there was always drama. I remember him coming to get me to take me places. It would start out being about our bonding time, but it would always end up being all about them, and their fighting. This push-pull dynamic between them increased the distance between us. More than that, it isolated me and paved the way for me to fall victim in this world where hurt people, hurt people. I was six years old, and I had so many emotions inside that I couldn't articulate back then. My mother found out that my father was cheating, so we were back at my grandparents' house.

I was happy because I was tired of the fights. I was always on edge when I was home alone with my parents. At least at Granny's house I could relax. I was free to be a kid again when I was at the house of love. It was structured and stable, with no confusion. At Granny's house I could always breathe freely. I knew what to expect...or so I thought.

This time around proved different. I had an extremely traumatic experience that likely caused me to go on an out-of-control roller coaster ride hoping to make sense of what happened (or maybe to dull my senses). I've never been able to shake what happened and I'm fighting to find the words to express it. It would be so much easier to just keep quiet like so many of us are taught, but I have to expose the truth because the lies that have been allowed to live have caused so much pain. It's these hidden truths that fueled my affinity for danger and self-destruction. They are what allowed me to hurt myself and others without remorse for so long.

One day I was playing outside with all my friends, my cousins, and their neighborhood friends. We ranged in age from six to about fifteen. In the words of Ice Cube, "[that day] was a good day." I was having the time of my little life. The mind of a child is so innocent. We harbor no evil in our hearts, so we can't see it coming. I had an older cousin who used to tickle me until I would almost cry. I hated it, but as a kid I loved the excitement of the chase and the attention. From time to time, as we all played that day he would come outside and playfully chase us around for a minute and then go back inside the house. He was older than us, probably about twenty. We were on Landon Street, about a block away from my sanctuary where Granny Love lived. On this particular day we were playing in front of my great great grandmother's house, grandma Pearl. She was a four-foot ten-inch unsung superhero, the kind of person they don't make anymore.

My cousin Tim, "the tickler" lived with her. He was a pudgy light skinned guy who was always kind of strange. He was a loner for the most part; no real friends, bad breath, body odor, and man boobs. People would pick on him a lot. He was typically ignored or avoided at family gatherings. He was a grown man, but most of his interactions were always with us kids. After running around outside for hours I got thirsty and went inside Grandma Pearl's house to see what I could get to drink. She was gone so all the kids (and the adult) were taking full advantage of her absence. We'd been ripping and running all around the porch and the backyard. When I ran inside the house I headed straight for the kitchen where I found some good old-fashioned lemonade, the kind in the big pitcher that was always in the fridge back in the day with real lemons and ice.

After gulping down my fill of granny's sweet lemonade, I was headed back out to play but I got cornered by my cousin Tim. He said, "Come here." He was in the doorway of his bedroom which was the last room one would pass before reaching the front door. I almost made it. He said he had something he wanted to show me. I was a little nervous because I thought he was going to tickle me, but he promised me he wouldn't, so I reluctantly went inside his room. He shut the door. When he closed that door, he also closed the innocent chapter of my life. I thought he tricked me. I started to tense up, so he told me to calm down. He said, "I just want to show you something, but you can't tell anybody." I thought he was about to show me some kind of secret treasure or something. I had no idea what it could be, but I was curious, so I agreed to keep the secret.

Then he said, "Look, if I wanted to tickle you I could," and he gently placed his hand on my stomach. I was apprehensive but his hand was on my stomach, and he wasn't tickling me, so I thought it was OK. He was keeping his word, so I believed him. When he saw that he had gained my trust and I was beginning to relax, he told me to close my eyes. This is when he took my trust and trampled over it. He took my child like tendency to trust and transformed it into a web of suspicion, cynicism, and doubt, a diabolical thing to do to a child. After this day, trust became a room I rarely entered.

He pulled down my shorts and my Superman underoos. I was scared and confused. I opened my eyes and tried to pull away. I tried to fight him off, but he held me tight, covered my mouth and told me to calm down. He attempted to reassure me by saying, "Didn't I tell you I wasn't going to tickle you? I just want to show you something. Calm down!" I was anxious and terrified, but I stayed quiet. By this time, I was retreating back inside my inner shell where I'd go when my parents were fighting.

I was petrified. I just stood still. He bent down in front of me and put my prepubescent private parts inside his mouth. I immediately pulled back. He stood up holding his penis in his hand and said, "Now you do the same thing to me." I pulled up my pants and bolted out the door. I ran out of that house and down the street to the place that had always been my sanctuary, my Granny Love's house. I wanted to tell someone what he had done to me, but by the time I got there I couldn't find the words. I started to feel guilty, dirty, and full of shame. The more I thought about it, the more I somehow convinced myself that it was all my fault. I agreed to go into his room. I promised to keep the secret. I could have fought harder. The damage caused by that one experience has been a demon that would fuel my future spree of reckless and rebellious behavior. It has been a cross that I've carried since that day.

After that day I tried my best to avoid him. I was determined to never be alone with him or allow him to tickle me ever again. I couldn't get what he had done out of my head. My six-year-old brain became consumed with sexual thoughts. I was at odds with myself. I questioned my own sexuality. I wondered what about me made him think I would like that. From that day forward I found myself doing everything I could think of to prove myself to myself. I never had any other encounters with this monster, but I still couldn't get it out my head. This one traumatic experience changed me. His were the hands that pushed me down the path of self-destruction.

A few weeks later another opportunity presented itself for me to prove to myself that I was a hero. My mom and her cousin Ronnie were fighting. My mom and Ronnie were around the same age, and they were always more like sisters than cousins. When I heard the commotion in the living room I put on my imaginary cape and charged in to save the day. I thrust myself in between them and in the midst of their tussle I broke my leg. It turned out that they

23

were just play fighting all along. I learned the hard way to stay out the middle of grown women's fights.

After getting my leg set in a cast my mom let me go spend a few days at my Cousin Mae's house. I loved everything about being over there. She stayed on Northumberland Street and being at her house was like being at an amusement park 24-7. She had three kids; Monique was the oldest, Shawn was the middle child, and Ebony was the baby. Although she had me by a few years, Ebony was the closest to me in age. We always played together and still to this day she's like my sister, my all-time favorite.

I loved going to Mae's house because when I was there, I instantly became the baby of the house, and she treated me like a treasure. At her house we could just be kids and get away with our mischief. Mae was a beautiful big boned, caramel skinned woman with big brown eyes. She wasn't educated, she could barely read, and she wouldn't be considered accomplished by society's standards, but I dare you to find a woman that loved harder than she did. Even today, she still has the biggest heart of gold.

Although my leg was broken, I was so happy to be there, and I was determined to have a ball. I was having just as much fun as everyone else. Despite my injury, I was hopping around, fighting, and trying to learn to ride a bike with no training wheels while wearing a cast on one leg. I actually ended up having to go back to the hospital to get a new cast. My mom was pissed, but she took it easy on me because she still felt a bit guilty for breaking my leg. I wanted to go right back to Mae's house. I don't think my mom really wanted me to go, but she knew how much fun I was having, and she never could tell me "No," so she just fussed a little bit and let me live my best life.

I had a little girlfriend named Mickey that lived on the same street, two doors down from Mae's house and my older cousin Shawn was messing around with her older sister. Mickey and I were just kids, but we looked up to Shawn and her sister. Shawn was like my big brother. I would do anything he told me to do back then. One night while Mae was at bingo, and we were home alone, we were tearing the house up, just having fun. Then all the other kids started to disappear with their boyfriend or girlfriend. Some left the house, others slipped into rooms to be alone. Mickey was about a year older than me. She was a pretty light-skinned girl with long jet-black hair. My cousin Shawn told us to go outside because we were too young for what was about to go down, so we went to sit on her porch when everyone did their disappearing act.

We sat there for a few, then we decided to sneak back into the house to see what was going on. We quietly crept into the house and right there in the living room we saw my cousin Shawn on top of

Mickey's sister. They were having sex or, "doing it", as we said back then. I'd seen this before. I was a six-year-old expert by then, so I knew what was up.

We watched them for a minute. Then I got a bright idea. I took Mickey upstairs with me and found an empty room. We took off all our clothes and started to kiss. We began to imitate what we had seen downstairs. I was only six, but I felt older, and this felt right. I wanted to erase the haunting image of "the tickler" from my mind. I needed to fill that space with images of something else. Preferably, something that would prove to everybody (but mostly to myself) that I was nothing like him, and that I didn't want what he did to me. I would go on for years engaging in behavior designed to communicate to others, and most importantly, to confirm for myself, that my sexuality was solid. I wasn't like him. Abuse is ugly. It hurts. Its consequences ripple and reverberate out in the lives of the abused, and there's no way to accurately predict how far those ripples will travel, or how fierce they will be. For some, the ripples just rock the boat, but I capsized.

Mickey and I had our first sexual experience together. We touched and grinded up against each other, and after a few awkward moments and a couple amateur pumps, I had an urge to pee. I jumped up and ran to the bathroom, and just like that it was over. I became extremely sexual. Looking back on that time, I now know it wasn't cute. I had been corrupted, twisted, turned into a little pervert. It was an indication of so many things to come, but there was no one around that recognized the signs.

I was exposed to so much, so young, and there was no way my underdeveloped brain could process it all. The cerebrum is the portion of the brain that manages our ability to reason, think intelligently, and problem solve; at six, mine was about fifteen to twenty years away from being fully developed. At the same time, my pituitary gland which regulates all normal bodily functions had been prematurely and perversely stimulated. I was a child living completely guided by my instincts, and not much else. I had no way to properly process the moans of my mother in the bed less than ten feet from mine, or the memories of a grown man's mouth violating me.

My intellect had not yet fully formed, so the chances of me doing anything intelligent in response to his attack were slim to none. The truth is, my parents were just kids themselves who still had a few more years to go before their brains would fully develop. This lack of parental maturity and structure is something most victimizers recognize and pursue when picking their prey. I make no excuses for the choices I've made; I seek only to highlight some of the mitigating factors that may help explain them. More importantly, my hope is that you take immediate action if you recognize some of the same factors present among your family.

After my experience with Mickey I was hooked. When I was with her (or anyone else) I was free of the guilt and shame that the boogeyman had bestowed upon me. When I was acting out sexually, I was suppressing the memories of what had been. In my mind, being sexual with girls emphatically answered all the questions this experience compelled me to ask myself, so I needed more... and I found plenty. I had no boundaries, like me, those had been broken. I didn't know what was off limits. The only thing I knew was that I had no desire to see another man's penis ever again.

I started experimenting with other girls who were around all the time. I know this is a taboo subject, but it is the truth. In fact, my years in prison have revealed that some form of childhood trauma and/or sexual exploitation is the truth for so many of us. So, being anything less than fully transparent in telling my truth would defeat the purpose of this book. As discussed above, children are very curious, but lack a fully developed intellect. They're often driven by instincts, observations of others, and a desire to be liked and accepted. Children are also eager to please those they love. When all this is combined with over exposure to situations that should be reserved for adults, you end up with children engaging in inappropriate and unhealthy behaviors.

This is dangerous. Parents must be mindful of what they allow their children to be exposed to and understand that exposure to people, places and things that are not age-appropriate makes children vulnerable to a host of negative outcomes, including mental, emotional, and physical harm.

I started to experiment with my girl cousins. We were doing things that make many adults blush. I can remember spending the night at Mae's house with two of my cousins who were about nine and ten years old, and they had also been exposed to entirely too much. We were all together in the same room and we were supposed to be sleeping. They asked me "to go down" on them. Once they explained what it meant, I was grossed out and refused. But they insisted and promised not to tell anyone, and I didn't want to be a punk. So, I did it to both of them. As soon as I was done, they both started to clown me. They laughed at me and said my breath smelled like "poontang". I was embarrassed and it would be a cold day in hell before a girl tricked me into doing that again. That was the first of many sexual experiences between the three of us. Who has a threesome at six? Me... that's who; a young man who would later spin out of control and receive a life sentence.

When I went back to school at the end of that summer my mind was completely occupied by sex.

I would flirt with girls and ask to see this or that. Show and tell became a private project that took place under the stairs. At this point I instinctively knew who best to approach and who not to. I knew how to spot the easy targets who had low self-esteem because they were damaged just like me. At the age of six I had been sexually educated in the worst way. It pains me to admit that the hands that tickled and traumatized me had also trained me.

I could have easily avoided this subject. I could have tried to clean it up a bit and make it pretty, but the reality is that much of my childhood was unseemly. As much as I would like to cover up this part of my story, I now know that covering these types of things up is what creates the space for them to continue. I should never have experienced many of the things I went through, but my mother was simply too young and incapable. She barely knew much about life and who knows what childhood trauma she was coping with. She wasn't capable of raising a child without making some critical mistakes along the way. It would be easy to blame her, but she was never the root cause, or the real reason for my future choices, nor was my father. The two of them did the best they could with the little they knew. Plus, I've played the blame game in so many of my life situations, and I know it's not a winning strategy. I've learned that it's easy to label someone, to judge them, to write them off, and move on, but what takes real work is seeking to understand, empathize, and address the issues without condemnation.

I could highlight more examples of what I was exposed to, as well as my own twisted behavior, however I believe the point on this subject has been made. This was a critical time in my life, and it caused me to set out on a new and disastrous course. I was no longer headed toward being a big hero, saving people from fires. Now I was the one who lit the flame. I was a walking inferno, ever ablaze in my mind and soul. I would spend years running from my boogeyman, not realizing I was becoming a different version of one, as well as my own worst enemy. It took years for me to connect the dots, and many people would become collateral damage in the process of me finding my way back to myself...back to the truth. My dream was to be a hero and I can only pray that by God's permission I can use my experiences to inspire change and possibly extinguish some of the fires raging in our youth before they are consumed.

CHAPTER THREE
Suffering Losses

B y the time I was eight years old my parents were finally done with their merry-go-round relationship. She moved out for the last time and did her best to move on. They loved each other, so from time to time they still had their moments, but they were done trying to make it work. While we were still living on Delaware Avenue my mom found my dad a job, so he stopped selling drugs. She had convinced a guy to give him a chance in his construction business. My father knew nothing about the business, but my mom persuaded him to give it a try. It turned out that he was a natural, great with his hands and a fast learner. Because he ended up being so good at his new job, he started taking jobs all over the place, so he was never around much. I only saw him on special occasions like birthdays, holidays, if a carnival was in town or when I was in trouble.

I could go weeks without seeing him, but when my mom called to tell him I was in trouble at school, he'd magically appear to whoop my butt. It was traumatic for me to go for what felt like months without seeing my dad, and then when he finally did show up, it was to beat me for being bad. I was misbehaving at school, and I did need discipline, it was just hard getting it from a "stranger" that I was afraid of. They didn't know it at the time, and I didn't realize it until years later, but my parents in adopting this pattern of behavior had actually set up a perverse incentive structure. In order to see my dad, I had to be bad.

He was a man that I saw hurt my mom in many ways, from physical abuse to emotional devastation. At this point, I had no meaningful connection to him. Even on days when he'd come bearing gifts and a smile, I didn't know how to accept his efforts. The thing is, I needed him. Deep down I loved him more than I knew how to express. I would practice what to say the next time I saw him (I still do), but when the time came, I could never get the words out. I would practice for hours, and I can count on one hand the words I actually said. I wanted to tell him what my older cousin did to me. I wanted to tell him that I missed him and that I needed to see him more. I had questions that only he could answer. He had stolen my security at five and I still hadn't recovered. In fact, I'd gotten worse. I hungered for a real relationship with him, but somehow my little heart instinctively knew he wasn't capable of being the man that this moment called for.

Back then my mom would rant and rave about him. She'd call him every name in the book, which didn't improve my own view of him either. I was one hundred percent dependent on her. Though she often made mistakes, she was the constant presence in my life, the one that I knew without doubt would always be there. I would listen to her words, and one by one those words destroyed him as a man, and his behavior didn't make it any better. To the contrary, his actions (or inaction) gave her words power. It didn't make them right, but it made them real.

What my mother failed to consider is that I didn't just look like my dad. I was a part of him. She conveniently forgot all the good qualities she fell in love with. Instead, she allowed her pain to rip him apart. She couldn't see that her words were simultaneously cutting me down as well. The more she diminished him, the more inferior I felt. After all, I was the sapling that sprang from this man's seed.

This became our norm. Time moved along and I saw my father less and less. Meanwhile, my mom became increasingly bitter, as it appeared that he was moving forward with ease, and not looking back. She felt like they belonged together; like she was the one who had made him into the man he was slowly becoming.... shouldn't she reap some benefits? I remember how she'd run down her list of grievances like clockwork, "I'm the one that helped that bastard with schoolwork. He could barely read and write. If it wasn't for me, he never would've graduated. I gave him a son. I dropped everything to take care of our family. I'm the one who got him that job. I begged them people to give his ass a chance. He'd still be doing nothing if it wasn't for me." The list went on and on. It unsettled me. Her words caused me to question who my father was, and more importantly, who I was and who I would become. The one thing I knew for sure is that I did not want to be anything like him.

I was a momma's boy. I loved her more than life. So, I didn't want to be like the man she seemed to hate. What she did not consider was how confused that left me. I didn't have many good examples of manhood. By this time all my uncles were either in prison, on drugs, or selling drugs. The one exception was my grandfather. He was a hardworking man; always there for us with no excuses. He was exactly the kind of man I now strive to be. Back then I was so consumed with thoughts of my father's shortcomings, that I never took the time to genuinely appreciate the greatness of my grandfather.

No matter what, I never blamed my mother. To me she could do no wrong. At twenty-two she was hardly prepared to deal with the complex issues I already had. In fact, she couldn't even recognize them. I was just another out of control kid growing up in a poverty-stricken broken home. I wasn't the only one. Where I'm from, I was the norm. My behavior didn't raise any red flags. To be fair, it's hard to notice a red flag when you're in a red room. The only thing that was raised were more belts to whoop my butt. At this critical stage in my life, despite the trauma I had already experienced to that point, there was still a chance. After all, I was a resilient kid. With the right nurturing from my parents and some therapy, my young mind could have been repaired. Unfortunately, my parents lacked the necessary tools. This is why it's so important for teens and young adults to understand that raging hormones, and "puppy love" are not enough to establish a strong family, or properly parent children.

In her immaturity, my mother turned my father into a weapon against me. He became the threat she would use to get me to "act right," never realizing the internal conflict it would cause for me. His actions, coupled with her words, had caused me to fear him and somewhat dislike him. Lost in her own pain, I don't think my mom ever stopped to realize I wasn't just her child. They were both blessed to bring me into this world together. They were both equally responsible for my nurturing. This was lost on her. In her mind I was her baby. She tried her best to be my mother and father but failed miserably. It was a fool's mission, one that could never be accomplished. A lie can never replace the truth no matter how well intentioned it may be. He was my father and both of them had a duty to see that he lived up to the title. The only thing she successfully accomplished was confusing me about who I was.

My father was not the best role model. However, he was the most important man I needed as a child. I needed my father like I needed water, but the more they fought the less I saw him. As I became more insecure about me, two things happened that likely changed my trajectory for good. First, I stopped wanting to be a hero when my friends and I played cops and robbers. I lost all interest in doing the honorable job of being a fireman. The sound of the trucks no longer fascinated me. Now my friends and I fought over who would be the villains. We all wanted to be the bad guys. I don't know if they had the exact same kind of issues in their homes that I had in mine, but I do know we all ended up on similar paths later on in life. What I am certain of is that from about the age of seven, I lost hope. I lost faith, and I lost my dream.

The second significant thing that took place is that my mother started to move us around a lot. We would live somewhere new and stay for several months at a time. I would meet new friends and then as soon as I was settling in, it was time to go. We moved countless times. We moved so much it's a blur. We lived in every neighborhood in the city of Buffalo. When we lived in Philadelphia for a few months with one of my aunts, I was awakened one day by the sound of my mother screaming.

She was standing up on our bed hysterically screaming. There was a tiny mouse stuck in a small waste basket. The mouse was struggling to get out, to no avail. We stayed on the bed for at least an hour hoping the mouse would flee. I fed off my mom's fear, so I was extremely scared. To this very day, I'm definitely jumping on the bed if I see a mouse.

After about an hour or more it was clear to my mom that the mouse wasn't able to move, so if we didn't, we'd be stuck there until my aunt came from work. So, we worked up the nerve to ease out our bed. She quickly grabbed a few of our items and we made a run for it. That was the end of Philly for us. We never looked back.

This was my life. It was unstable. We'd move from place to place with pit stops for a few days, weeks, or even a few months in places like Washington DC, Baltimore MD., Atlanta Ga., Richmond Va., and Camden NJ. But when it was all said and done, we'd always end up back at 85 Landon Street. It was the only place I could ever really call home. My father was very passive when it came to being in my life and my mom had all the control. It was her way or no way.

She had full control to torture my father by keeping me from him while at the same time conditioning me to believe he was a no-good bastard that did us wrong.

I started to blame him for everything that was wrong in my life. I acted out in every possible way. I became a class clown in school. I would rush to finish my schoolwork just so I could act a fool in class. This was the period where the change that had been festering came to full fruition. With few exceptions, up until then, I had exhibited some bad behavior here and there, but for the most part, I always listened to my mom and did what I was told. Despite my occasional bad behavior and unstable upbringing, I always had good grades and good manners. I was quiet and shy. In fact, up until this point, I had to run home from public school 53 every day because a kid named Walter used to bully me. Every day he promised to beat me up after school. Walter was big for his age. He looked like a mini version of Mike Tyson. I had to run home and keep it a secret because my mother would've kicked my butt if she ever found out I ran from anyone. She had strict rules about that. Darlene's doctrine was that you never run from a bully, even if they're bigger than you. My mom's advice would be to pick something up and defend yourself.

So, becoming the class clown, talking out of turn, and being disruptive was all new for me. One day I remember going to school with a plan to beat Walter silly. I got some brass knuckles and after school instead of me running home I walked the opposite way towards the back of our school. He followed me like always, talking about what he was going to do to me. As I walked, I slipped my hand in my book bag to get my weapon. It was time to stop this bully. We got to the back of the school, and he said, "I got you now!" I turned around with my brass knuckles on and said, "Let's Go!" When he saw I had no fear and that I was prepared to fight, he backed off like a coward (which bullies typically are). At this point I was ready for whatever. I wanted to fight anyone now. I had just punked the person most people in the school were afraid of. From then on, I was a fighter (which is different than a bully).

I started getting in fights a lot, and found out I was good at it, which only encouraged me more. I became a problem at home. I went from my mother's respectful, smart, and handsome son to this demon child. This overnight transformation was a sign; one that went unread. I would do the craziest things and my mother would beat me. Then she'd call my father, curse him out, and make him come whoop me too. After a while I became numb to it. I just wanted it over so I could get on with my day. His beatings had no substance and did nothing to deter my path or disrupt my patterns. So what if he was upset or disappointed in me. I felt the same about him. Who was he anyway? I felt like he didn't care about my feelings, so beatings from him felt like abuse; not love, genuine concern, or discipline. After all, he never took the time to try to figure out why I was acting this way. This made me angry. It made me resent him even more.

Every time my mom called him, I felt betrayed. I thought it was the two of us against the world, especially him. He was the enemy. He was the reason we were moving from house to house. I even blamed him for the abuse I suffered at the hands of my sick and twisted cousin. Why was she calling him? Why did he only come around for birthdays, holidays, and beatings?

Sure enough we moved again. My mother thought it would do the trick. She thought moving would get me away from my friends and force me to meet new people, but in the back of my mind I knew that as soon as I got to know them, we'd be moving again. I was livid. I had no intentions of embracing a new school or any new friends with open arms. My plan was to make my mom's life a living hell until she moved us back home. Eventually I got my wish, but not before I met my future ex.

Being away from home had me upset. I had a chip on my shoulder. I had a million emotions I was dealing with that I didn't understand. It was in this madness that I remember first laying eyes on her. She was nine years old; I was eight. The first day I saw her I was in awe. She was such a little lady; unlike any other girl I had ever seen. She was the first girl in a long time in my short life that I respected. I wanted to get to know her. From the age of six I had been treating girls my age and older like objects. I was trying to get thrills so I could erase the ugly image of my pedophile cousin stealing my innocence. Then there was Nickie; I wanted to marry her. I barely knew how to spell the word love, and I sure didn't know its meaning, but somehow, I still knew instinctively that whatever it was, I had it for her. Sadly, when it came to her, I was my old shy self again. Anytime I was around her I couldn't find the words. I'd practice what to say the next time I saw her, but Just like the song, "Come and Talk to Me", by Jodeci, every time I got my thoughts together for the very next day, when I saw my little lady, I'd forget what to say.

Then, as if on cue, we moved again. It was OK though because my uncle Steve owned a record store around the corner from where she lived, so I had an excuse to go over there. My uncle Steve was technically my mother's first cousin, but they grew up like brother and sister. He was Granny Love's sister's son. My great aunt Tilly died when I was about four. All I really remember about her is that she was a diva. She worked hard and played even harder. She was the type to wear expensive furs and jewelry. She's the person my mom got her sense of style and love of fashion from. When aunt Tilly died My Granny Love looked after Steve and his sister Mae like they were her own children and my mom treated them like siblings.

When Aunt Tilly died, they were both young adults, in their early twenties. and she left them all her valuables. She left her car, some money, and her expensive furs. Somehow, after the funeral was over and the dust had settled, all the money was gone, someone had stolen the furs, and the only thing left was a car they couldn't afford to put gas in. So, my mother and Steve came up with a plan. They successfully staged the car being stolen and burned so Steve and Mae could get the insurance money. The money came and Steve morphed from a square to a drug dealer. With my mother's help, he was introduced to all the right people, and eventually became one of the biggest drug dealers in Buffalo. What he also became was my role model. At this time, it was one tragedy after another for me. I lost my aunt, then I lost the illusion of who I thought my mother was. Day by day she was becoming someone else. On top of that my cousin Antwan, who was a year older than me, died in a house fire. He was one of my running partners. Our crew consisted of my cousin Ponny, my friends Jason aka Jay-Bird, and Antman aka Pop-Dog.

Around this time my mother started to get deep

into dating and Darlene didn't date just any kind of guy. She had a type. She consistently chose the kind that shouldn't be around a kid. They all fell into one specific category, unavailable street dudes. After my father, my mother became unavailable herself. She was more callous. Her heart was still with my father but she was determined to never be hurt again. So, she dealt with men for one reason; what they had to offer monetarily. This exposed me to other harsh realities. My mother's choices and behaviors taught me not trust women. I lost respect for them in a different way. I was already objectifying them due to my own twisted thinking and now those thoughts were being confirmed and validated by my own mother's behavior.

She became cold and calculated towards men. She saw them as a means to an end. I have a vivid memory of a caper she pulled when we were living on Nevada Street in Buffalo. Although we had everything we needed, she moved our furniture, our stove, and refrigerator out the house and then one by one she called various men who wanted to be with her and told each one the same lie, line by line. I watched her literally crying, telling them she didn't know how she was going to take care of me or feed me. Each one gave her money to get what she needed. After they all left, and she was satisfied, she called her brothers to bring everything back. The crazy part is not one of those men were ever invited back over to eat one meal made from her stove, or to get one cold drink out the refrigerator they thought they bought.

Another standout memory is when we were staying in a house directly behind my grandparents on Riley Street. It was early in the morning and my mother had company; a man named Ron. I didn't know it at the time, but my parents were still involved with each other. My father came knocking and I let him in. He caught her sleeping in bed with Ron. My dad was furious, he started swinging on Ron. He beat him until he went running down the street naked to his own house. Next, he turned his violent rage on my mother. I ran through the shortcut in our backyard to my grandparents' house to get help.

With all this craziness going on I was a mess. At that time, the only silver lining in my dark cloud of a life was Nickie. There just were no words I could find to express it. I would go around her but each time I would lose the nerve to even speak. As a result, she started to be insecure around me. She thought I didn't like her. So instead of her becoming my childhood sweetheart, we became distant from each other for years. I was almost nine years old. I was in love in my head with this girl I couldn't even say "hi" to. I was mourning the loss of family members as well as being exposed to my mom's dark side. I could've become anything in life. All I needed to do was overcome the rough start. But honestly, by this point I had lost my will. I was on course to take a long and hurtful journey through life. Losing my dream, and my stability crippled my chances. The obvious losses I could have possibly recovered from, but it was the injuries that went undetected that set the stage for my future performance.

CHAPTER FOUR
My First Love Affair

I t would be nice if I could say it was Nickie. If it would have been that simple my life would likely have had a much different path. However, she remained only a wish back then. My reality was much darker. My first love is the one who has broken my heart countless times; she's the one for whom I've gone to dark places and done the darkest things. My first love affair was with money. I fell madly in love with it and the power attached to it. I loved the praise I got from others when I had it even at a very young age. As my uncle gained more and more success in his life as a drug dealer, I was waiting in the wings observing it all and falling deeper in love each day.

The police called my uncle Steve "The Six Million Dollar Man". On the one hand it was a reference to the popular 1970's TV series because my uncle Steve had the same name as the lead character. On the other hand, it was a recognition that Steve was ostentatious and flashy. His lifestyle was the epitome of ghetto fabulous. I witnessed firsthand how the atmosphere changed when he walked into a room; Uncle Steve was the man. I was too young to know much about the character from the TV show, it was before my time, but "The Six million Dollar Man" that I knew and loved kept a bank roll in his pocket, truck jewelry around his neck and wrists, and shiny white luxury vehicles for cruising around town.

This man commanded everyone's attention. Both men and women begged to be noticed by him, and when he held court, opportunities to have a word with him were highly sought after and coveted. Steve was only about 5'8' and maybe 190 pounds. He had a Jheri curl that was medium length and a memorable chipped tooth smile. To those that got to know him, he was amazing, and capable of changing your life. To others, he was more than that. To me he became a god. The original name of the record store he owned on East Ferry Street in Buffalo was J and E's records, which stood for the names "Jennifer" and "Eric." Jennifer was his girlfriend and Eric was one of our cousins. Eventually, Eric saw that the record store was really a drug front, and he wanted out, so the name was changed to include that of another cousin. The name changed, but the game remained the same.

Before long the record store became a main attraction and center of activity for family, friends and about two or three real customers. The actual purpose of the store was to provide a safe place to conduct business where the true commodity could be camouflaged and go unnoticed due to the mixture of traffic, and the veneer of legitimate business. The record store became my hangout spot where I was able to see a more in-depth example of what I only got a glimpse of at home. I was in love, and there was no turning back. My destiny became very clear to me. This was the life I wanted for myself. I started taking notes. I was done with being a kid anyways. I was simply waiting for my moment. The problem was at nine, I had some growing and a lot more learning to do.

I would often stay over with some of Steve's kids at a house he had with his girlfriend, Jennifer. We would have lots of fun. It was like a big clubhouse. There was never much supervision, just kids watching kids. On one of the many occasions that we were there together, one of Steve's youngest sons told us a cool secret. He knew the combination to Steve's safe. We were curious to see what was inside. We all went into the room and got the safe open. We were amazed by its contents. His sons didn't really know what they were looking at. They knew it was drugs but not much else. For me this was very familiar. I had seen this for years. Only this time it wasn't just a passing fascination; this was my future. I wanted to have a safe like this, and I wanted what was inside.

The safe was filled with all sorts of things. We had no idea of its value, but I recognized the green leafy stuff. I suggested that we take some of the marijuana and sell it. They thought I was crazy, but I had a plan. I had been paying attention, waiting for my time to come. So, we got the courage to steal some of it. I was determined to be loved like Steve. I wanted and needed that power, no matter the cost. This was my entrance into the game.

It didn't take us long to complete our first transaction. I told my cousins about these girls who were always around the record store getting drugs from Steve. I had no idea how much he charged them, I just had a feeling I could get them to buy it from us and keep it a secret. One day I called them on the house phone and told them I had what they wanted. I realize now how stupid I must have sounded to them. The saving grace was the fact that we were Steve's boys. So, they told us to come by their house. My cousins were scared. I was exhilarated. This was my destiny. It was like a gravitational pull. I had no choice. We went to their house, and when they saw that I had it and that I was serious, they paid me. I pushed my first pack at nine out of pure instinct, but I'm pretty sure they beat us, and continued to do so for weeks.

The way they called us handsome, flirting with

us like we were grown men reminded me of how I observed Steve being treated every day. I had to have this life; I couldn't live without it. I was head over heels in love with it all. We were stupid, and sloppy kids so it didn't take long for our operation to get shut down. We had been sloppy with going into Steve's safe to steal more product and he got suspicious. The problem was that there were a lot of us. Steve had a bunch of kids so there was no way to pin-point who was the culprit. Even now we don't know how many kids he had; our last known count stopped at thirty-three.

His solution was to bar all of us from coming over until somebody told who was going in his room. Nobody folded, we all kept our mouths shut. And just like that, we lost our connect, and had no way to supply our growing clientele. By the time he let up on his restrictions, it was too late. His safe was no longer valuable to us; when we went back inside it was empty. We never found anything in it again except some dirty pictures he didn't want anyone to see. We got some cheap thrills off of that but not much else. We were so disappointed. We were counting on being able to get back to work, but instead we were back to square one. For my cousins it wasn't that big of a deal, but I was heartbroken.

My cousins came up with other mischievous ways to get things and I would tag along, but I wasn't into stealing. It was just never my thing. The truth is, I was a spoiled kid (and so were they). If I wanted something all I had to do was tell my mom and she would figure it out, or finesse it, but I always got whatever I wanted. At that time what I really wanted was to be like Steve. I wanted the power, the adoration, the respect and you don't get that from being a sneak thief. I was miserable ever since our caper got busted up. I didn't understand why, but I felt like I had to have the clout and reputation that Steve had. I felt like I needed it to live. The sad reality about this kind of godlike adoration, the fast money, expensive things, and all kinds of people at your disposal is that it comes at a high price. And it's not just your expense; it's also costly to those that love you. As men we aspire to be gods, and to be praised as such. Yet we lack the foresight to see all that comes with such a weighty responsibility. Especially when your road to reach such heights is illegal and void of any lasting security. I got to see this up close in a very personal way.

It was Christmas Eve, 1989. I was at my Granny Love's house. It was the most beautiful time of year as people say. Steve came to the house, it was about 10:00 p.m., I'll never forget this night. My Granny Love was up late finishing preparation for the family's big Christmas meal the next day. Steve came in for a minute, he left his new all white pathfinder running in front of the house. The music was playing low, because he always turned his music down before he got to the house. Otherwise, you could hear him coming from blocks away because his system was so loud. After hugging my Granny Love and giving her whatever he stopped by to drop off, he was headed out. She stopped him in the hallway at the threshold of the front door. My idol stood there like a King, draped in gold. She asked him where he was going, and he told her he had to stop by the bar. He said he was going to a bar called the Tanqueray, which was on East Ferry Street, and then he was going home. She said, "Steve, it's Christmas Eve. Go home. That bar will be there tomorrow." He said, "I know Aunt Sylvie I just need to check on a few things, it won't take long." My Granny Love told him again, "Please, not tonight. I've got a bad feeling. Just go home to your kids and save it for another day." She made him promise he would go straight home, and he promised.

Despite the promise made, Steve went to the bar that night instead and some guys tried to kidnap him. It was supposedly payback for him not coming to the rescue of a woman in his company one day. Apparently, their theory was that she got hurt because he didn't intervene. These men tried to forcibly escort him out the bar. There was no way my uncle Steve was going out like that so there was a struggle, and he was shot. Subsequently, after months of fighting for his life in the hospital hooked up to all kinds of machines, my uncle Steve died. This destroyed our family, and so many others that loved him. He had two unborn children on the way. So many people depended on him and at the age of thirty-one he was gone.

This was a lesson for all of us, especially me. It made me angry, and more determined. The loss of such a big life created a void in the lives of so many in my community. Someone had to fill that void. This would prove impossible, but many tried. He was the reason everyone in Buffalo, and other cities knew the Austin name. He was the reason most of us lived, dressed, and ate good. Bills were paid and families survived because of this man, and now he was gone. The irony is, in the near future I would go on to cause others the same pain and devastation that losing my uncle Steve caused me. It's only as I write these words that I realize, "I'm sorry", even when it's sincere, is never enough to the loved ones of a murder victim.

Again, the void was great and needed filling. My mother indirectly became the person people looked to. They looked to her for ideas, for some sense of direction, and predictably she failed. The truth is, and always will be, that there's simply no way to replace a person, or fill the void left behind after their death (especially not a person with a life as vast and as vibrant as Steve's). Our family was going through many forms of grief. There was blind rage that resulted in acts of retaliation against people that had nothing to do with his death. Others slipped into denial and disillusion; they started abusing drugs and alcohol, and the list goes on.

For me I had a mixture of all the things I was exposed to. My mother began to do many things that I observed, and learned from as she made her own adjustments out of anger. She was doing all she could to manipulate people to carry out her will. Which was pretty clear, she wanted the people responsible for his death to pay the ultimate price for it. She also started to sell drugs more openly, exposing me to it even more. At the same time, she spoiled me rotten with things. Even when I did wrong, she still spoiled me. As I look back now, I understand that in her mind, I literally could do no wrong.

About two years had passed since my first drug deal at nine. For a child two years seems like forever, especially for one who couldn't wait to be grown. I was in a rush more than ever now that my role model was gone, so it shouldn't shock anyone that at eleven I was doing everything I could to break back into the business. I would do almost anything to get my hands on some drugs to sell. I would steal my mother's cocaine and take it to the neighborhood drug boys. I would sell to them and literally take whatever price they offered me. They loved to see me coming because they knew I had no idea what I was doing or what I had. In all honesty, I was just satisfied with how they ran to me and treated me like I was important. I felt like the man. The money was just one aspect of the power I craved. I also wanted the affection that came with the money. When my mother found out that I was standing on street corners with the drug dealers she would beat my butt like there was no tomorrow. She would call my father and they would take turns beating me. But there was no stopping me, I would take my beating, wait for her to let me off punishment, and then I was right back at it.

She even put me on probation and threatened to send me to a group home for troubled youth. I called her bluff, but when the time came, she didn't have the heart to put her only child in the system. So, she did the one thing she always had the heart to do... move. We packed up again and headed to a different neighborhood. She always thought moving would fix our problems. Just like all the other times, it didn't. As the saying goes, "No matter where you go, there you are." I was now going to school on the south side of Buffalo, and I met another kid that was just like me in so many ways. He was about a year older than me, and in a similar living situation. His pops was a big-time drug dealer, and my new friend was a troubled kid who wanted to be like his pops. Unlike me, he wasn't being discouraged at home. This was great for me; I found a person I could hang with that my mom would think was safe. She had no idea who his parents were. She was just happy I wasn't trying to sneak back over to the Coldspring neighborhood every day. She could not imagine that the first friend I met would be the son of a major drug dealer that actually had no problem with his son selling drugs.

She did not understand, this was my destiny, there was nothing, or no one capable of getting in its way. My new friend, Mone, and I got started going straight from school to Strauss and Sycamore to sell crack cocaine every day. I would help with the sales, which is when I learned the real value of the merchandise. I realized I had been getting robbed. I made a few dollars, but it was not the money that kept me coming back. It was the knowledge, and that was priceless. It was fun while it lasted. After a while my mother realized the truth. She was in the game, and she knew almost all the major players in the area. I was banned from Strauss and Sycamore with the quickness; she made sure of it. Once Mone's father found out who my mother was, it was a wrap. I was no longer allowed over there.

Unfortunately, she was missing the point. It wasn't where I went, or who I hung out with, the problem was me. She had convinced herself that if she just changed the atmosphere around me, that would change my actions and objective. By the time my mother pulled her head out of the sand to truly see what was happening and who I was becoming, it was literally too late. She was in deep denial. She thought there was no way I could have remembered or been able to understand the things I was exposed to as a child. She thought I had no memories of playing on those bean bag sized garbage bags full of marijuana at the age of five. She thought I believed it was actually a beanbag. She refused to see herself in me. She was never a sucker, so how could she have raised one. Of course I knew what was going on, even as a kid.

The lies we tell ourselves to rationalize our actions can be blinding. At nine and ten I can remember her distributing vacuum sealed one-ounce packages of cocaine to her workers to sell. She allowed herself to believe I didn't grasp the reality of it all. The truth is, I not only fully understood, but I also fell head over heels in love with the lifestyle. My mind was made up, I was going to be the next major hustler from my family. So, at that point she could have moved us to Africa, and it wouldn't have mattered. Wherever we went I would have found a way to continue my first love affair.

CHAPTER FIVE
My Coming Out Party

I can clearly remember June of 1991, a little more than a month away from my thirteenth birthday. It was the end of the school year and I felt beyond ready to embrace my fate and become "the man". I was tired of being a kid and pretending I would grow up to be anything remotely close to what I dreamed up for myself when I was a child. I had fifty dollars to my name. I had stolen the money the night before (me the guy who didn't want to be a thief). I took it from the purse of a family friend while she was visiting my Granny Love's house. She left it hanging out of her purse, and I took it without thought. When the theft was discovered, they blamed everyone but me. To my Granny Love, I could do no wrong, so no one dared to suggest otherwise at the time.

I left early the next morning supposedly to go to school. At the time I was in an alternative school for troubled kids. I left that morning determined never to come home. At least not as a child or a resident. The next time I came back to that house I would be a man or a visitor. It was time for me to spread my wings and fly. I was ready. I could do it. I left with only the clothes on my back, and the stolen fifty-dollar bill in my pocket. My aim was to find a viable way back into the drug trade, and to be the next godlike figure of the streets of Buffalo. My mind was consumed with thoughts of shimmering jewelry, and flashy cars like the one's hustlers around my way and my Uncle Steve had. I got about a block away before I started to get scared. I didn't know where I was going or what my next move was. At this point I had never purchased a drug. I had only stolen drugs from family and sold them with a friend. So, I did what was familiar. I started walking back toward Strauss and Sycamore where I used to be with Mone, but as I got closer, I realized I would likely be turned away. I was lost, and unlike the past this was different, the stakes were much higher. I was now technically homeless with no food, no clothes, and no clue how I would change my new self-made reality.

I was walking up the street in my neighborhood on Wholers street. I saw this kid I casually knew at the time named Shamel sitting on his porch. As I approached it was apparent, he was upset. I greeted him, asked him was he going to school, he said, "No". Then he started telling me that he was mad because his mom wouldn't buy him any new sneakers. He told me his birthday was coming up and went on about his frustration. In listening to him I immediately knew that I had found an ally. So, I told him about my own plans, and how I was done with the school stuff. After sharing my plans he let me know that he had some of the missing ingredients needed for my drug kingpin recipe.

I wanted in the crack game but had no reliable sources for product. I had that little bit of money to purchase some drugs and he knew where I could get it. It was just my luck (or so I thought). These guys in the neighborhood were selling double ups. Which meant they would sell you prepackaged drugs worth double your money. As soon as he told me about it, I was in, and off we went to the drug house. We got the double up, I gave Shamel half, and we became business partners. We chased down clientele, going back and forth all day to get double ups while kids our age were in school. By the time school let out we had made enough money to stop buying double ups. We moved up the ladder, we promoted ourselves to purchasing eight balls (an eighth of an ounce) which cost us a hundred and twenty-five dollars back then.

We needed a new connect to get the eight ball, and Shamel knew a guy. We paged him and he called us back pretty quickly. We made the deal and ended up with an eight ball each. Shamel was able to go to the sneaker store on Allen Street called Rick's and get those new sneakers. We were hooked. It was easy, and there was no turning back for us. I often look back and wonder who was more addicted, the user we sold to, or the buyer they bought from? There's no simple answer. Both sides could make a legitimate argument against the other. All I know is nothing could have stopped me after that first day. I was officially a full-blown drug dealer, and I was addicted.

Day turned into night; we had been on the clock for hours. Now the reality of my situation started to sink in. I had no place to stay. I left home early that morning knowing I would not return, but not knowing where I'd go. Looking back, it was a pretty stupid plan. I was a wounded child, and my actions were very telling. Sadly, no one responsible knew how to identify what these actions were revealing. I was born to two children, dead smack in the middle of one of America's worst neighborhoods. I didn't stand a chance of being noticed and rescued from my own actions that were rooted in pain as well as fear. In these impoverished communities we're not born with the luxury of being allowed to develop in a "normal", and healthy way.

In society as a whole, boys are conditioned not to cry; we're told to suck it up. If we cry, we're called "girls" as a way to disparage us and attempt to minimize our masculinity. This is a cultural issue that needs to be addressed. Combine this with an environment where there are a multiplicity of other issues, like poorly educated parents and family, extreme poverty, substance abuse, exposure to domestic violence and gun violence, absentee fathers along with many other disfunctions and what you get is young men (and women) like me.

These dynamics make it impossible for a child of any age to be seen and meaningfully engaged. They make it difficult for parents and family to identify, and focus on fixing problems that may be presenting, and even if noticed, the resources necessary to effectively help are non-existent. In these impoverished communities, if you start behaving in a way that should be a sign to adults that you need help, what you typically get instead is something that often causes more harm. It definitely is a hard knock life. Instead of treated, we get tracked into "special class" also known as the prison pipeline. Instead of counseling we get kicked out of school and exiled to alternative schools and group homes where you just learn more dysfunctional behavior.

This leads to the next step, court ordered supervision by a probation officer; now you're on the road to advancing your criminal career. There was no room, time, or resources available to properly deal with troubled youth in my community, and from what I can see, not much has changed. There are too many of us, and so few people that actually care. So, instead of playgrounds, afterschool programs, and community partnerships, tax dollars built prisons and they were filled with kids like me.

This was the backdrop when I found myself at the age of 12 on my own with more money in my pocket than I had ever had. I didn't know how to manage it, or what I needed it for, but my other pocket was full of poison. Even though 85 Landon Street was in my heart and had always been home, I couldn't stay there anymore. My pain, my need to prove a point and my desire to get away and become "the man" would not allow me to go back. My newfound best friend told his mother he wanted me to spend the night. She asked all the questions a mother should ask. She stated the obvious immediately about it being a school night. We told her every big lie we could think up with our little brains. She gave us that knowing look, she knew we were lying. She knew I was on the streets and should be home. She also knew if she sent me home, I wouldn't go.

In communities like mine it's common for people to have to make the best choice out of several bad options. So she chose to let me stay. Her house wasn't technically my home, but she knew it was a whole lot better for me than the streets. Her house might not have been home, but at least it was safe. I fell in love with that woman that night. I started to call her Ma Duke. She became my other mother and I have loved her as one ever since. Ma Duke was pretty cool. I would send her to Canada for bingo almost every day. She loved going and she won a lot, but she never let us know how much. She'd just get us a big pizza, so it was like a pizza party for us every night, nothing but love. Some nights I would stay, others I would pretend I was going home, but I actually hustled in the street all night long. I had a goal. I was chasing down money and infamy. If nothing else, I would be hood rich and famous.

Looking back on it now, the other side of this story is even more heart wrenching, I was just too foolish to understand back then. I couldn't see the big picture. I wasn't thinking long-term. I left home one day at the age of twelve to go to school and never returned. I wasn't from a family void of love; in fact, my family loved me beyond measure. Before I left, I was living at my Granny Love's house so when I didn't come home from school that day my family had no idea if I was even alive. I didn't call, I didn't leave a note or a clue. I just left. As the days passed, eventually my family learned where I was, and what I was up to. I hadn't gone far. I was still in Coldspring where my whole family was well known.

This time my mother decided to take a different approach. I'm guessing she started to realize that she had exposed me to this life and began to wrestle with her own guilt. She had two choices. She could try to discipline me and correct my course, or she could choose to create a totally new and abnormal dynamic in our relationship. Had she tried to discipline me, I think she may have been able to slow down my rapid slide into the depths of street life. But again, she didn't have the proper tools to prevent or impede my progression. I believe she intuitively recognized that I was too far gone for her to fix and in that moment, she reluctantly made the second choice. She decided to create a different type of mother-son dynamic.

I remember I was out doing my thing on the corner of Wholers and Northampton. Out of nowhere this five-foot ball of fire rolled up on me. My mother scared the piss out of me. My heart sunk down to my shoes. I knew I was in serious trouble, and I braced myself for the incoming blows. Reflecting back, there was a part of me, (the part of me that was still an innocent six-year-old boy) that was waiting to be rescued by her. I needed her to come to save me from my own madness. I needed her to figure out what had happened to me; and here she stood. I was terrified yet happy at the same time. She was my true hero, and I missed her. But instead of popping me upside my head as I expected and deserved for disappearing, she immediately dispelled my concern.

In a tone that was shockingly calm and deliberate she said, "Don't worry I'm not going to hurt you, I should, but I'm not". Then, after easing my mind she rocked me worse with her words than she ever could have with her hands. She said, "You know you look like a whore standing out here on this street corner. Who you out here selling yourself for?" I was taken aback, but I gathered myself and tried to protest but she cut me off with words I'll never forget, "I know I showed you this life. It's not your fault, it's mine. I may not be able to get you to stop because it's what I showed you, but please come home tonight so I can talk to you, and show you a better way".

I told her I would come to the house, she looked at me as if she didn't know if she could believe me. "Dee please come by the house, if you're going to live this life you need to do it right. You look like a whore out here and you come from better than this." I promised I would come. She had my attention, especially when she called me "Dee." That day she embarrassed me in front of my drug dealing comrades which was a small thing compared to what else her words had done. More consequential than the public humiliation was the private realization that my hero wasn't planning a rescue mission. She had destroyed any secret hope that she would save me. This was my life and not even my own mother was trying to stop me anymore.

That day I remember a part of me felt like I won. Over two decades later sitting in this cage, I know it was at that moment that my losses started to come to full fruition. That night I went to my Granny Love's house. I waited until it was late because I knew my Granny Love would be upstairs in bed. I lightly tapped on the window, my mother was up and waiting. The two of us were a bit uneasy at first seeing as the dynamics of our relationship had changed. We were no longer simply mother and son, now we were professor and pupil, mentor, and mentee. When it came to the street life and the drug game, she was a Jedi, and I was her young padawan. When it came to a hustle, the force was with her (and the fruit don't fall far from the tree).

I was weeks away from my thirteenth birthday, yet I was there to talk to my mom about how to be a better drug dealer. She was going to try to teach me how to survive in a life where there are no survivors. She was not about to teach me how to do my homework or how to treat my first girlfriend. She was about to do her best to give me the tools to survive in a lifestyle she felt hopeless in keeping me from. In her mind, this was how she would save my life.

I can imagine what you're thinking. "How could she?" I can feel the judgement. "What kind of mother would do such a thing?" Those in my family that knew her best are upset by my candid revelations. For those of you that want me to water down the truth, I want you to know that if we could afford to, I would. But our community's lies, cover-ups, and buried secrets are much too costly. This is my story, and she is my mother. There are simply too many who need saving; so, I will not hide at their expense. And you cannot expect me to. For those of you who dare to judge her, make sure you also dare to save.

Try to understand the dismal plight of these impoverished communities before you simply label, condemn, and discard. In these impoverished communities we have many secrets, and our youth have been the price we've paid in order to keep them. Our children are being prepared to fail and instructed on how to fail on a high level. What does a child with a child do when it's time to be a parent? What happens when that child starts to have psychological issues from traumas the parent does not understand? Let's go back even further, what happens when the parent has her own psychological issues at the same time as her child? Who teaches the children if the people responsible have limited or no education? No medical coverage, living in poverty, dealing with a thousand issues too complex for anyone to ever want to make the effort to sort out. Who deals with all this? The typical answer is, well they should keep their legs closed. I always find this alarming, one sided, and short sighted. Young women in the hood are humans too. They have desires like all other young people. What they don't have is the proper education, creative outlets, and family structures to temper those desires and balance out the naturally impulsive behavior of youth.

It's always easiest to judge something you haven't experienced, and don't understand. When it's time to imagine new ideas for change, or to assist in some meaningful way those same voices disappear. The masses run for cover, shut their doors and whisper about the unfortunate. God warns us to be careful of the whisperer. The truth is that the solutions are as complex as the problems. For most it's easier to simply judge and move on. This is why our prisons were built, and why they're often overcrowded while our schools are often empty.

That night, my mother gave me what she had, and I'm grateful. If she hadn't, instead of writing this book I would've been in my grave twenty years ago. Admittedly, she didn't choose the best course, not because she didn't love me or want the best for me, but because the best was unavailable to her, and you can't give what you don't have. So, she gave me what she had and what little she had helped me survive. I will forever be grateful that she didn't allow her pain, disappointment, and shame to make her run, hide, and quit on me. She is my Rock Star. There are a great number of mothers out there faced with the same dilemma with even less to offer their own children. As a result, the news is filled with stories of our dead. Our children are dying and coming to prison as if it's an amusement park. This has to be addressed in a much more effective way. We have to do better as a society, and it starts with us knowing better.

I left the next morning after staying up in the late hours of the night with my mom. She told me her pain, her fears for me, her mistakes with me. She let me know she didn't want this for me. She begged, she pleaded, but she did not demand. She knew her son, instead of playing the fool, living in denial, and burying me early, she introduced me to a high-level dealer that she trusted. He was someone who was moving right, so he could show me how to play the game without making all the typical mistakes that land people in prison.

She did what she could and so did he. I just failed to listen to their instructions. I was a hardheaded kid, nothing could change my course, and I was on a deadly one. In the coming days I became bold, I was aggressive, and more determined to own my moment. My mother had given me some instructions and made me give my word I would stay off the corner. She showed me how it made me a target for police and stick-up boys looking for easy targets to rob. I took all her words to heart on this particular point.

I started forcing my way in other people's established drug spaces. I became a bully in my approach, and it was working, which only encouraged me even more. I remember one of my older cousins had a friend who told me I couldn't sell drugs at his

71

drug spot. He told me I was blocking his money and I had to go. I went to the gas station and created a Molotov cocktail. I came back and firebombed his house. If I couldn't sell my drugs there, no one could. I had to make sure my point was made with more than words. I wanted everybody to know Lil Dee was not the little kid they used to know. I wasn't just one of them either. I had plans to be more and earn my respect. After that incident I was the talk of our neighborhood. To some it was funny, but others were scared. They didn't know what I'd do next or how to treat me. Some avoided me, others befriended me. The guy whose house it was went and told my Granny Love. She didn't believe him, and told me about what he said, which upset me. My Granny Love was off limits to my reality in the street. I told him to let that be his last time telling her my business; and I meant that. In time to come, he would cross me again and learn the hard way just how seriously I had lost my way.

CHAPTER SIX
True To Her Word

As I stated, my mother had not just promised to teach me things, she promised to provide certain resources. A few weeks had passed since that pivotal conversation with my mom that had shifted the shape of our relationship. I steered clear of the corners like she instructed. I was finding other ways to make money and it did help limit my exposure to the competition and to the cops. Then out of nowhere this guy that lived in the area who I'd seen around stopped his car in front of me as I walked down Wholers Avenue. It was a brand-new gold BMW which he rarely drove. He was usually in his old beat-up looking car. I didn't think the BMW was his because to me, why would anyone ever drive that beat up car if they had a beauty like that gold BMW? I was naïve and had no clue. This enigma of a man rolled his window down and asked, "Are you Lil Dee... Darlene's son?" I told him I was. He asked me to get in because he wanted to talk to me.

Initially I refused until he explained that he was doing her a favor. I got in and he drove in silence for a while, it was calculated on his part. After several moments pregnant with anticipation, apprehension, and excitement, the real lessons began. This man showed me the art of the drug trade and revealed that I knew absolutely nothing. He showed me his method from the ground up. Over the next few weeks he taught me many things, and over the years, from the age of thirteen until well after my arrest, the lessons continued. To be clear, my lessons weren't just about selling drugs. He was teaching me how to be a man among boys in the life I had chosen. I refuse to say his name, I would never want to cause him any harm or bring any unnecessary attention his way. He always worked extremely hard to avoid attention, so I will not violate that boundary. I can say for certain that besides God, and my mother this man is the only other person I can credit for helping me walk away from my life of crime. While I wasn't able to escape my extended stay in this state administered gated community, thanks in large part to him, I was able to escape a premature grave.

I didn't know exactly what my mother told this man, or what influence she had over him that got him to take such a risk and an interest in me. I had never seen him around our family or around her.

He wasn't a well-known dealer to me, in fact, when I saw him, I never associated him with crime at all. This man was an enigma, and he was offering me the expressway into the upper levels of the game. His only requirement was that I do it right, which was also my mother's directive. He paid someone to teach me the chemistry of the substance I was selling. He gave me cocaine and told me to have this specific lady cook it up for me to transform it into crack. Unbeknownst to me, it was a set up. He had paid her in advance to beat me out the drugs.

When I came running back to him complaining that what he gave me was no good, he took me back to her to teach me how she beat me. Once that lesson was learned my coursework continued. I moved on to advanced level classes. He instructed her to teach me how to cook it myself, so I could never be beaten again. By thirteen I had dropped out of school, but I never stopped my education. I just changed subjects and traded in public school for private tutoring, and I was well on my way to being a scholar. I was a fast learner and before long I knew how to do every possible thing one can do with cocaine.

Although I was receiving a top-notch education in the drug game, that couldn't keep me from being a kid and making plenty of poor choices with my newfound freedom and sought after skillset. I wasn't satisfied with learning the valuable lessons I was being taught, like how to stay out the street, off the radar, and out of the limelight. I was too young, stupid, and shortsighted to become exactly what my heart desired. Instead, I was in the streets making a name for myself, remember, I wanted to be "the man." What was the point of being "the man" unless everybody knew it. Most of my choices at that time were actually counterproductive to my ultimate goals and completely contradicted the things I was being taught.

When my mother told me I looked like a whore standing on the street corner, it created a lasting impression, and I developed a complex about being a corner boy. I was better than that. I was Darlene Austin's son. Whenever low-level drug dealers offered me drugs to stand on a corner and sell for them, I felt highly disrespected. So, instead of selling drugs for them, I would take drugs from them and refuse to pay them their cut. For the most part I got away with it. They just took the loss and never dealt with me again.

I thought I was tough. I had no idea how my actions were hurting me more than them. It would all catch up to me eventually, one way or another. Their maturity and experience allowed them to see farther than I could, so they understood that what I was putting out would someday come back to me. From their point of view, there was no need to start a feud with a stupid kid who had less to lose than them. They gave me a pass, which only emboldened me. I had a battery in my back. I thought I was untouchable, so I did it again, but this time my target wasn't the type to give passes. We ended up in an altercation that got the attention of my mentor, the man who made avoiding attention an artform. My blatant disregard for the rules and general attitude of invincibility had brought heat his way and he refused to be associated with anything that caused drama and attention.

I had become a liability. This dramatically altered our level of interaction, and I ended up losing much more than I gained by not paying what I owed. I had told the guy I would pay, so in my mentor's eyes, if I couldn't keep my word on a two-hundred-dollar agreement, how could I be trusted on something more? I couldn't see that far, and I didn't think it through. The very actions I was engaging in to try to build a reputation for myself, ended up costing me my reputation and I was too young and dumb to see it coming. My mentor kept me at a distance for a while. Without his guidance, I started to lose focus in significant ways. I was still making money, but I started mixing business with pleasure. Predictably, these major distractions started to cost me time and money. I was getting a lot of female attention, more than I could manage, naturally drama ensued.

My girlfriend at the time, Cee Cee, lived in the Langfield apartments on the other side of town, but she would pop up in my hood without notice. This caused all kinds of problems. I'd have to run and hide. Shamel would cover for me and tell her I was gone or make my side chicks leave. I was tired of it and planned to fix it, but before I had the chance to make things right one of life's curve balls came hurling my way. There was a girl named Robin who was always coming to my neighborhood to visit her friends. She was eighteen years old and already had two kids. She had a caramel skin tone, with a voluptuous video vixen body. We started messing around and I was hooked on her body, and everything else. I lied about my age, and we were having sex every chance we got, anywhere we could.

One night I was walking her home, and we ended up on the side of a Church. Thank God before we went too far, we realized where we were. With the way we carried on, there was no surprise when she ended up pregnant. I was too stupid to be scared, she was more experienced. She already had two kids; she already made this mistake. She also noticed how I would run when Cee Cee would show up. So, when she learned she was pregnant she started asking me questions she had learned were important. I had none of the answers she wanted to hear. She told me she was not going to have more kids by a guy who wouldn't be there as a partner. I made every promise I could think of to assure her that I would take care of my kids no matter what. She was pregnant with twins and insisted my promises were not good enough. She asked me if I would be with her, and if I would I get out the streets. At that age I was foolish, and bold, but with very few words in my vocabulary. And there was simply no way I was about to give up the streets or settle down. I told her that she could just have my babies and give them to me, and they would be fine. I stopped asking and started demanding.

She eventually told me what I wanted to hear, and then went behind my back and got the abortion. She had my cousin Ebony tell me what happened. I can't even pretend that this news didn't knock the wind out of me. I was angry. I went looking for her, but it was too late. She knew I was a loose cannon. Robin made sure she was nowhere to be found. I never saw her again, and still today I often think of what I lost. This pain motivated me to refocus and grow up a bit more. It also caused my heart to grow a lot harder. I became ruthless in the streets and avoided the familiar neighborhood for a while. I started to hang around one of my older cousins. He's one of the shadiest, untrustworthy people you never want to meet. He showed me how to get in real trouble and how to do it without remorse. Let's just call him Shady.

Losing my twins and my response to that loss pushed me way off the path my mom had set me upon. It would be a long time before I found my way back to anywhere near what she had in mind for me. Now that I was exposed to and comfortable with the harshest realities of the streets, I fell in love with a new power...guns. The power of guns was even better than money because money created fake friends in your life and invited vultures to come hunting for you. With money it was impossible to distinguish between family, friends, and vultures. The lines blur, and in the midst of the obscurity, you become the prey. But with the gun, you're the predator, and the praised. Of course most only pretended to praise me out of fear, but this was better than pretending out of greed, and larceny.

This is where I must be clear, no one forced me on this particular path, or fully encouraged me to take it. I simply got a glimpse and took to it like a fish to water. Reflecting back on it now, the honest to God's truth is that I had an angry edge ever since I was touched by that monster as a child. In my mind, it was my own fault, and I swore to myself that I'd never let anyone corner me again. I was determined to protect myself. Sadly, what I actually did was avoid facing the pain which just made me more vulnerable to other things. In my extreme effort not to be victimized ever again, not only did I become a continuous victim, ironically, I became my own biggest victimizer. It was my very own hands that caused me the most damage. I was so adamant about not being hurt that I hurt other people. In reality, there's almost no one I hurt more than I hurt myself.

I was obsessed with carrying a gun with me no matter where I was, or what I was doing. There was one occasion when my Granny Love insisted that I go to Church. She made me promise to go. So one Sunday morning I went. I got to the door and realized I had my gun with me. I couldn't go in there like that. This was my dilemma, in the back of my mind I knew that if my uncle Steve would have listened to my Granny Love, he would still be alive, so I always followed her directions and never second guessed her; but even I couldn't go inside Granny's church with a gun in my pocket. So, I decided on a happy medium; a way to keep my promise and maintain the sanctity of the church. I sat on the side doorstep of the Church and listened to the full service outside of one of God's houses of worship with my trusty gun in my pocket.

It got so bad that I built a reputation in the streets and with most of the local cops for being someone who had a gun at all times. Every time the police saw me, they pursued me, and if they could catch me, they always recovered a gun. Because I was underage, they didn't bother processing me through the system, mostly they'd just take my gun. Plus, if they charged me, they'd have to voucher the gun as evidence, but if they just took me home to my mom there was no paper trail, so they'd get to keep it for themselves. It sounds crazy, but whenever I got caught with guns the cops would often make a comment about how I was just a kid, and my guns were better, newer, more expensive, and powerful than theirs.

Sometimes they would take me to the precinct until she came to pick me up. She would always show up for me and always say the right things to the police. Once we got outside, she would ask me to come home. My answer would always be the same. I would always break her heart with how determined I was not to return. Heartbroken, rejected, and beaten, she would still give me advice, make sure I knew she loved me, and make sure I knew she wanted me. Then she would assure me she would always show up for me when I needed her.

Many months had passed since Robin's abortion. I was hanging in the Doat and Burgard area hustling. I was staying away from my old neighborhood. I had learned from my mother that moving away was an acceptable coping mechanism. I had never seen it solve her problems, but it's what was familiar. What Robin had done hurt me in many ways that I didn't understand. One of the typical signs of a kid who has experienced serious trauma is their strong desire to have their own child or create their own family. We believe that we can get a "do over" through the child. We want to prove that there is a better way to raise a child than the way we were raised, and that we're capable of getting it right. At the time I didn't recognize why losing my children hurt so much. I just knew it did. I had learned to run, so that's what I did. While in this new part of town my cousin Shady took me to meet his new girlfriend. Her name was Angie, she was beautiful, and had the sweetest heart. I didn't understand then (or now) what she ever saw in him. Whatever it was, she was really into him and I gave him his props.

By this time, I was fourteen years old, I had been in the streets for well over a year, and I guess I looked the part. Because I was able to convince people there that I was eighteen. With sober, better-informed eyes there was no mistaking the fact I was still a boy trying to be something I wasn't. But they only saw what I projected. I met Angie's sister that night, her name was Star. She was just as beautiful as Angie, but she had an edgy side to her. She was less reserved, raunchier in speech and how she presented herself. I enjoyed the meeting, but I was ready to get back to my new sanctuary, the streets. I told my cousin I was ready to get back to it and Star overheard me. She asked me to stay a bit longer to hang out with her. She offered me some beer that she was drinking heavily. I declined the beer, telling her I didn't drink or do any drugs. My addiction was of another kind which I thought I had figured out. I was a sucker for a pretty face, so she convinced me to stay. I still had zero thoughts of anything being possible between us. She was a grown woman, twenty-two years old at the time. In my head she was out of my league. I didn't even consider the thought, but before I knew it, aggressive and inebriated, she invited me to have sex.

I was nervous. Who am I kidding, I was terrified. But we went to Angie's daughter's room and all I could think about was the fact I was really still a kid. I was inadequate, as soon as I undressed, she would realize I was just a boy. But I still had to do it. I couldn't say "No." I was in the streets. I had been confronting all types of fears worse than this, and each time I went in headfirst. Why should this be any different? There was no turning back. I wasn't going to tuck my tail and run home to mommy because I couldn't handle it. So just as I always did, I played the part and had sex with her. To my surprise, she appeared to enjoy herself, and that led to us being in a full-fledged "adult" relationship. She was naturally aggressive (even sexually), and I learned on the job. We became inseparable, I moved in with her and without noticing or intending to I had stopped hustling in the streets. I was caught up, learning how to be a man in another way, and it appealed to me. She had two kids, a boy name Brandon, and a girl named Gail. I fell in love with those kids, we started to live the family life and I was the man of the house. I always wanted to be "the man" I never imagined it would be like this.

We settled into our own routine. She even stopped drinking because I didn't like it. I had a beautiful woman, two beautiful kids, and a great sex life. Happy ending? I wish. But there was no way my demons were done, and I was far from done making foolish decisions. My cousin Shady came over one day wanting me to go somewhere with him. It was around Christmas time, and I had just taken the kids with me to take pictures at the mall with Santa. Despite Star's protest, I went out with him. I should have listened to her and stayed away from him. The night ended with me in custody for a carjacking case. This was a serious felony. There'd be no sending me home with my mom this time. Instead, I was sent to juvenile detention. The case even made the newspaper. The jig was up, I was in juvenile detention, the story was in the news and now Starr knew that this whole time she was playing house with a fourteen-year-old boy.

She was devastated, I was busted in more ways than one. But my precious mother was always there, even if I didn't deserve it. She not only showed up to court, but she made sure the complainant never came. The charges were placed on an open calendar in case the victim surfaced, but we all knew they never would. It was over. The bad news was that Star felt betrayed, like I played her for the fool. I didn't know how to face her. I was embarrassed. I loved her and didn't

85

want to give up the fantasy family we built together. I went home to her; she had been drinking and was emotional. She asked me all kinds of questions; she was trying to understand. I told her a bit of my story, but not what was driving me. We stayed together, but things changed.

The new dynamic was Darlene. Star had spoken to my mother who convinced her to agree to something I didn't like. I hadn't been to school in months, the streets were teaching me all I was interested in learning. My mother hated it. She was a lot of things, but a dummy wasn't one of them. She knew the power of education and was adamant about me getting mine. She could learn to accept and maybe even respect some of my unsavory choices, but being uneducated was unacceptable. She told Star, "If you're going to be with him fine, but do not let him lay under your roof during school hours becoming a fool, send him to school". This was crazy to me; my mother was employing my girlfriend to do the job she no longer felt qualified to do.

I reluctantly agreed to go. At first, I was going, and it was alright, but eventually, I realized that this was not what I wanted. School made me feel like a kid again. I was used to having money in my pocket and now I was broke and being taken care of by Star. I couldn't live like this. I had to make something happen for myself. My mother was my "go to" in all things whenever I was in trouble. So, I went to see her and told her that I was broke and needed her help. She cursed me out and asked me why I hadn't kept in touch with my mentor. I had no excuse, but it was pride, which always shows its ugly face before the fall.

She was very upset. It was one thing to accept that I was doing certain things. It was even okay in her mind that she indirectly aided me. But now I was asking her to go beyond her limits. I was asking that she remove the delusions she had created in her mind to justify her choices and her passive assistance with some of mine. I was literally asking my own mother to give me drugs so I could get on my feet. This was too much for her and I was too ignorant to recognize it. She couldn't do it. There was no way she could hand me a plastic wrap of crack cocaine. But what she could wrap her mind around was giving me money, so she handed me some cash and told me to do what I wanted with it.

She refused my initial request so she could tell herself that she never actually gave me drugs, but we both knew that was a lie. She had just given me drug money so that I could go and buy drugs to make more drug money. She definitely knew that I was going to take that money and use it to buy exactly what she had refused to give me. Either way, I was back in business. Instead of going to school I went to the Doat and Burgard area to sell drugs. I was hiding what I was doing from Star like she was my mother. The high that comes from getting fast money selling drugs soon consumed me. Before long I was spending most of my time in the streets. I wasn't home much so Star thought I was cheating. She was on my case; our fantasy was finished. It was now friction and consistent arguments which soon escalated to physical confrontations. I had been taught well to never hit a woman regardless of the circumstances. Despite what I had witnessed as a kid, I refused to adopt physical force as a tactic. Unfortunately, I was with a woman who had a predisposition to using physical force to communicate her displeasure.

Whenever I came home, she would smell me, and if I smelled different than she thought I should, it would be a problem. I really wasn't cheating; my mind was on reaching my goal. I had lost focus with her. At that time, I was trying to figure out how to be with her without losing myself. This was proving to be impossible. After she punched me in the face one night for coming home with lipstick on my shirt which was left there by an innocent hug with a relative, I started staying away even more. She teamed up with her sister Angie, who was her ride or die and they both came looking for me. They came to the block and found me standing on a corner (exactly where my teachers told me never to be). Star jumped out of a car they had stolen and hit me in the face like

I was one of her prostitutes that ran off. The irony of the situation was not lost on me. My days of standing on corners needed to stop. I had to figure out a better way. I grew tired of the drama, and I knew I had to end the relationship.

I loved Star, but at the time I didn't love anything (including myself) more than I loved all the perks and the power that came with selling drugs. It wasn't an easy break up. She actually held me at knife point trapped in a corner of our bedroom. She told me I was not leaving her. After a long intense stand-off, her sister Angie was able to convince her to let me leave. I ended up in the streets again. I was staying in a drug house that my cousin "Q" had with two of his longtime friends. They reluctantly let me become a part of their operation. We all had shifts when we worked the house and kept the profits. They really didn't want me around for obvious reasons, but against their better judgment, I was allowed to be a part of the team. Things were going great; I was making more money than I ever had up to that point. Then this young kid (ironically, we were about the same age) kept begging to be given some drugs to sell. No one would even think of it because he was a known gambler. His only interest was shooting dice for money. He had a gambling addiction, so everyone refused.

He started to focus on me. I told him he was too

young, and that he needed to go to school. I told him to stay out of the streets and gave him a speech. The whole house laughed at me, of all people, telling him to do what no one could get me to do. In my mind, I was different, this was my destiny. I had no choice, the universe had spoken, this was my life. I was trying to make sure he didn't end up making the same mistakes I had made. I had no way of knowing at the time that my life had not even started yet. Having a chance to change was a foreign concept to me. I couldn't see it for me, but I was begging him to see it for himself. Instead, he pointed out that I was not much older than him, insisting he was ready and able to handle it. He finally broke me down and I agreed. Everyone warned me not to do it. I told them, no I'm going to try him out. I warned him, "If you mess up my money... I'm going to shoot you." He promised he wouldn't mess up and gave me his word that he would do the right thing. I said, "just remember I begged you to go to school and get out the street, if you mess up my money, I'm going to shoot you. I don't care about your age, you want to be in the street, and not go to school, I'm going to treat you like a man."

I gave him ten bags of crack; it was worth a hundred dollars. The deal was he keeps forty percent, I get sixty. I told him he would get more if he showed me he could handle it. Although the speech was directed at him, the words were for myself, and the child trapped inside my madness. I was just too far gone and there was no one that could get through to me; not even the little boy inside me who wanted to go home and grow up to be a fireman. When the kid left everyone told me I was stupid. He was not going to pay; I should just count it as a loss. I told them with no doubt in my mind that if he played me, I would make him wish he went to school. They thought it was a joke. I secretly hoped he wouldn't make me have to show him that I was all out of jokes. I was in the cold, harsh streets and I was playing for keeps, but this wasn't child's play. That kind of playtime was over. I didn't have any G.I. Joe toys in my hands. I had crack cocaine in one and a gun in the other. This was real life, with real consequences. No one, not even the boy in me was about to stand in my way.

The very next morning was my shift, and I was at the house alone. The kid came knocking and I was glad to see him. "You got my money?" I asked. He said, "Dee I messed up. I need you to give me something else. I had the money, but I started playing dice. I was winning, then I lost everything." I let him in and locked the door behind him. I said, "Take a seat." Before he came, I was playing a video game. I sat down, took the game off pause, and continued to play. Then I said, "I begged you to go to school. I told you this was not for you, but you didn't listen." He tried to interrupt me, I said, "No, you listen, I told you that you were too young for this. You begged me, you promised you could handle it. When I gave you my shit, I told you if you didn't have my money, I was going to shoot you."

I paused the game, took the 380 handgun out simultaneously removing both safeties from the trigger and hammer. As he began to plead, I pulled the trigger. I shot him in his chest, fear combined with adrenaline propelled him to run out of the house and collapse in the street. I knew he would tell what happened, and where it happened. I realized too late that I had made a mistake. I had to clean up. There were drugs everywhere. I took what I could and left the house. I didn't know where I would go, I just ran. I ended up on the train tracks, I hid the gun, drugs, and triple beam scale. Then went home to my mother, she would know what to do. I caught a cab to my Granny Love's house so I could talk to my mother.

She immediately knew something was wrong. She took me upstairs and told me to tell her everything. When I hesitated, she said, "boy I'm your mother, I'm always going to be on your side. I can't help you if I don't know what happened. You can lie to everyone but me, tell me what happened so I know how to help you." I told her everything, and in seconds she knew her next move. She turned me in to the police. I went kicking and screaming. I could not believe this was her idea of help. She assured me that it was the only way. She said the boy would tell, and the police would come right to Granny Love's house looking for me. She walked me right in the precinct and told them I was the one that *accidentally* shot my friend. She told them I ran away scared and had thrown the gun on the train tracks. She even gave them a different set of tracks to search for it. They took me in custody and sent me to the juvenile detention on East Ferry with the worst of the worst.

By this time, I had been arrested for three guns, and a carjacking. I was on my way to being a career criminal. I spent three days there; my mother made some calls, and I was moved to a better place. The new place was more like a halfway home for kids. We were allowed to go home, and we were taken to the movies by staff on weekends. I was upset, this was not what I had in mind, my mother kept telling me to trust her. She never gave me a reason to doubt her, so I had no choice. I spent eight days in this two-story house, went back to court and I was ultimately released. I never had to return to court, and only a few know all the details of how she made it go away; and I'm not one of them. All I know is that my mother was always true to her word when it concerned me. I don't know all her reasoning; I just know she was a better person to me than I was to her. When I shot that kid, in a twisted way I was shooting myself, my anger, and my disappointment. It wasn't about him or that sixty dollars. I was trying to kill whatever innocence I still had in me. I was tired of hearing that little boy in me begging to go home. Somehow, he needed to die in order for my pain to manifest into the monster I was becoming to be able to survive in the streets. The innocent kid and the callous criminal could no longer coexist. So, in a way, that was my first suicide attempt.

CHAPTER SEVEN
Now They Fear Me

After that incident blew over, I didn't go back to the area where it took place. I was back in Coldspring, and a lot had changed since I was last in my neighborhood. For starters, the location to make money for our crew had moved. The new spot was on Riley Street, which was right around the corner from Granny Love's house. This was a little too close for comfort, plus it was another corner, so I didn't like the idea. At the same time, Ma Duke, my second mom had been saving the money we'd been giving her to help her buy a home. Between what we gave her, and the money she won at bingo, she was able to do it. One summer day she picked me and Shamel up and took us to see the house. To us it looked like hell on earth, we thought she'd lost her mind. There was no way this place would ever become livable. She was determined to teach us a life lesson while proving us wrong.

In the meantime, money had to be made. With so many changes going on, I had to figure out how to make money. I also had to do it in a way that my mother would accept. I decided that I would do what my friends were doing, I would just be more careful. I was hardheaded and didn't know what good advice was. My first day out on the block trying to reestablish myself with the customers, I played myself. I got beat like a rookie for some of my drugs. I had been gone for months, so even though this was my neighborhood, I was the new guy on the block. This had me anxious to make my first sale. The older dudes on the block were giving me props because I just came from juvenile detention for a shooting. I was the man of the hour; everybody was looking at me differently. It felt like I was getting more respect. This false sense of security had me moving sloppy. When this customer pulled up in a U-Haul truck, three people rushed to the truck, all trying to make the sale. There was no order, it was every man for himself. I decided to bully my way in on the action, and the customer, not recognizing me as being from around there, decided to teach me a lesson. He told everyone, "I'm going to deal with young blood right here," referring to me. I was talking mess to my boys like I was the man because he picked me. They walked away; he had a handful of money. He told me to show him what I was working with. So, I took my biggest ten dollar bags of crack and stuck my hand in the window to show him. He hit the bottom of my hand, causing my product to fly out my hand and land in his lap. Then he put his foot on the gas and sped off before I could respond.

The whole block start laughing and clowning me, saying, "That's what you get!" I was on fire. My fragile ego was not built for their mocking. I told them to stop playing with me, and next time I saw that fool I was going to kill him. They kept laughing, disregarded my words, and told me it was my fault. I should have known better. I did know better; I wasn't even supposed to be out there on that corner like a two-dollar hooker. I thought I was smarter than I was. At the same time Shamel and I were being forced by Ma Duke to come with her to Smith Street every day to help clean and fix up the house. The two of us were trying to make money, not work on a beat-up house we thought had no potential. So, we came up with a plan, we found two drug addicts and offered them jobs. We promised to pay them every day that they showed up to help her. This way we were off the hook and free to get back to work. We tried to make money over there, but we were unknown in the area, so it was hard. Plus, Ma Duke was paying attention, she told us she didn't want us doing that where she was trying to build her first home. So, we would walk around looking for other outlets.

Eventually, me and another friend from the neighborhood came up with what we believed to be a promising spot on Lyfe Street. The money was good. The set up was great. I can still remember the smell of the place. It smelled like smoked crack. The aroma emanated from the resident of the house we took over. Back then that smell reminded me of money, so I liked it. Out of nowhere my partner in this place got arrested for beating one of his classmates to death. I was devastated. We had so many plans, we were about to do some great things as far as we were concerned. There were so many rumors as to exactly what happened, but for me all that mattered was that he was gone. I was hurt. Every possible plan was blowing up in my face. It's almost like God was trying to tell me something; but I definitely wasn't trying to hear it.

I went back to Lyfe Street a few times, but it wasn't the same without him. I ended up back on the corner of Riley Street. This was where my friends were, but any excuse would do. I just needed to be around my crew at any cost. Things were cool for a minute; maybe two. Then this family from Lackawanna moved to Landon Street a few houses down from my Granny Love. They started selling drugs out the house. This had everyone upset, not only were they strangers to us, but they were selling for half the price. This was killing our business, and no one liked it. I came up with a plan to get them out. No one wanted to make a move on them without knowing anything about them. I was too stupid to be worried about who they might have connections to. So, one night I planned to spray the house up with bullets. A few people tried to discourage me while others were eager to see if I had it in me. I was creeping through a short cut to Landon Street when I spotted a familiar face. The same guy from the U-Haul truck weeks earlier. This was perfect; almost everyone he played me in front of was out there.

He pleaded with me when he saw me. He told me how he later learned that I was an Austin, and my mom is Darlene. I had to credit him for doing his research. Then he swore once he found out my pedigree, he had given my money to my cousin Shady. I didn't believe him; my cousin never said a word. Hindsight tells me the guy was telling the truth; my cousin was just a scumbag. But at the time it didn't really matter, even if he did give the money to my cousin, what about my pride? I gave him five seconds to run. He thought it was a joke. When he heard me start counting, he turned to run, and I shot him. I didn't stop to think how this might prevent me from successfully completing my initial plan of getting that family out the neighborhood, which it did. I was upset because I really wanted to get rid of those people. I didn't know them, and didn't even know why I was doing it. What

I did know is that I started to like shooting a gun, not just having one. It wasn't long before I got my next fix.

The way it felt in my hands, and knowing the power I held was addictive. So, when Pootie disrespected me on the block in front of everyone there should have been no doubt what I would do. In his eyes I was just a kid he had known since I had snot running down my nose. He used to give me change for the store. He couldn't see past the little kid he used to know, so he tried treating me like he used to. He was one of the few who hadn't gotten the memo, but today was the day. I went around the corner to Pootie's best friend's house, my cousin Shady, and got his gun. I didn't tell him what for, and I went running around the corner. It was a beautiful summer night so everyone was out on the block, which was perfect. When Pootie saw me, initially he didn't move, but when he noticed the gun, he started running. I chased him into a yard where he begged me not to shoot him. I aimed for his face and pulled the trigger. The bullet hit him in the shoulder as a result of his defensive maneuvering. I tried to shoot a second time, but Shady was soon upon me snatching the gun before I could get a second shot off.

When I look back, there was no reasoning in my brain. I was on autopilot. There was no reason to shoot him, especially in front of about a dozen people. That man was a longtime family friend. Yes, he had been disrespectful in my eyes. Especially when he told my grandmother I firebombed his house the year before. He even insinuated that he was going to tell her I was on the corner that night. These were all minor infractions, none of which warranted his death. In truth, he had a right to want better for me and to try to discourage me from continuing on that path. Had I been able to reason, this would have been an easy conclusion to reach. But again, the reasoning part of my brain was far from being fully formed at the age of fourteen. I was living on instincts and operating on survival mode. In my underdeveloped mind he was a threat to the survival of who I was trying to be. To him I could never be more than a snot nosed kid. I had to figure out how to rearrange his perception of me so that my reputation could survive.

My instincts compelled me to get rid of the problem. I was tired of running from it, tired of being seen as Lil Dee. I had to destroy that image. So, when this happened, and the block was filled with witnesses, I felt that was the best time to kill that man as well as his perception of me. I didn't see all those people on the block as possible witnesses in a court of law. I saw them as witnesses to me becoming more than a boy to be played with. They were there to witness the death of the kid known as Lil Dee so "the man" could be born. I couldn't see it back then. I had no way of understanding that I was subconsciously doing my best to destroy myself. In my fragile, uninformed mind I believed I was an animal, so I acted like one.

In many ways I got the desired effect. I was no longer the kid "Lil Dee;" I was just plain crazy. People called me crazy to my face with a smile. "Boy you crazy!" Behind my back the tone and the tales were different. I became the person no one really wanted around, but no one dared say it. Fear was always better than love in the streets and there was no doubt I started stirring up fear. I didn't expect it to spill over into my own friends and family, but it did. With my new exhibition of violence and viciousness I wasn't just killing an image, I was killing relationships. My best friend, and brother from another mother, Shamel was being encouraged by Ma Duke to stay away from me. My infamous reputation was growing by the day. I was working overtime to build it. Shamel loved me, but in his heart, he was not like me. He didn't have the same drive to destroy his past as I had. He wasn't running from the same darkness that I was.

One day he told me he was moving to the Carolina's with his grandmother. He didn't have the heart to tell me I was the catalyst for this sudden change, but I knew. When we met that June day a few years prior when I found him sitting on his porch dissatisfied with life, both of our lives changed. There was no doubt in anyone's mind that I played a part in his change. Up to that point he hadn't gone as far in the deep end as me, so his move was a prevention effort. Everyone knew if he stayed, it was only a matter of time. I was on my own, all I had was a growing reputation, and my deeply rooted pain. In my mind everyone was to blame but me. I was a ticking time bomb. They had a right to fear me. If I were smart, I would have been scared too.

After Shamel left I became a miniature version of what I was with my mom. Moving from place to place. I was everywhere, searching to fill a void that had been empty ever since I could remember. I had a rapidly hardening heart. I was as uncertain as I had ever been. As time went on, my father's appearances were fewer and fleeting. I think it was because he didn't want to deal with the reality that his only son, his namesake, was out of control. It was easier to just avoid me, this way he didn't have to confront his own missteps or how he contributed to my miserable condition. This made it that much easier for my heart to grow in its bitterness. My mother on the other hand was different in her approach. She loved me regardless and did her best to stay involved. She kept communication open with me. When analyzed, it was all fear based, my mother, father, extended family, and friends, all acted out of fear for me and of me. I became so unapproachable that people just conformed to my will, walked on eggshells around me, or looked the other way.

I became a master of giving the impression that no

CONFESSIONS OF THE ACCUSED

one or nothing could change me. Fear led everyone to buy into the crap I was selling. None more so than me. I was getting high on my own supply of pretense, and fabricated persona. I don't care how many drugs I sold, or how many guns I shot, deep deep down, I was still a boy. All I really wanted was some attention from the right source. I wanted my parents to recognize my trauma, rescue me, protect, and nurture me. I was screaming to be noticed, and with each passing day of those screams going unheard I became a bit more broken. It became easier to pretend, easier to fool those observing me. I was a method actor. I didn't break character. I became as convincing as any award-winning actor. Denzel and DeNiro had nothing on me. This was my academy award winning performance. Sadly, the award for being so good in this particular role would be a fate no child should ever endure.

CHAPTER EIGHT
One More Chance

Make no mistakes, my mother was no pushover. She's one of the strongest women I have ever known. In no way do I intend to paint her as helpless, or weak; she was far from it. So, after she watched me make a mess of my life, while doing her best to guide me without alienating me, she decided to take a page out her old book. Against my protest, she told me I was moving to Virginia. She is the toughest person male or female I ever encountered. She didn't ask or beg, so I went with her. Secretly, I wanted and needed a change. By this time, I was fifteen and hadn't had the type of phenomenal success in the drug game that I had envisioned. It's not as easy as it looks. There were many more problems than money involved. I didn't anticipate the problems; all I saw and all I wanted were the glamorous parts. At that point I had experienced very little glamour. Nothing like I had witnessed from my idols. The cars, jewelry, and real money had been elusive, but the problems had been plentiful.

We went to Richmond Virginia with one of my mother's good friends, Patty. My mom had a close family friend down in Virginia named Gene that owed her a favor. She had helped him make some valuable connections when he came to Buffalo on business. He was glad to return the favor and help us get settled in hopes of changing my path. He also had a thing for Patty, which is why my mom brought her along for the trip. He arranged for us to stay with his sister until we were able to get our own place. I soon learned that Gene also had his own room in the house although he didn't live there. I hated it from the start. There were no kids my age, and nowhere for me to go. The one area across the bridge where I had seen a housing project with a basketball court was off limits to me. Gene told my mom it was a bad area and under no circumstances should I cross that bridge and go over there. As I'm sure you can imagine, any place that was off limits was also intriguing. It was calling my name. I was on lockdown, and ready to go home. I was there for about three days with nothing to do but observe my new surroundings.

I noticed that Gene would go inside his padlocked room every time he came over. He always went into his room alone. No one was allowed inside, and he always made sure to lock it back immediately upon leaving. He wouldn't even go to the bathroom without that door being securely locked. My instincts told me there was something in there. As the next few days passed, I was waiting for an opportunity to have a look inside. One night he took my mom and Patty out on the town. When I was the last person awake in the house I went to work on the door. I soon found the padlock was too hard to manipulate open without damaging the door. At first, I decided to give up. I didn't want to damage the door just to find out there was nothing in there worth my trouble.

I laid back down and was thinking about the type of business he was in while in Buffalo. My mind was made up. I went back to the door knowing there was no way I was not getting into that room. There was no doubt in my mind that there was something worth having in there. I forced the door open with total disregard for the damage I might cause. I took a moment to listen for movement downstairs; when there was none, I went inside. I found the light and was immediately disappointed. It was a room full of what appeared to be junk. There was no order at all, just a bunch of old worthless furniture. Then my instincts said he was hiding something major in there. I went on a treasure hunt. I found many treasures and was soon overjoyed that I had decided to persevere.

I found diamonds, Rolex watches, gold chains, and more diamond rings. I could tell it was all real. I even found bullets which piqued my interest even more. I was ready to leave but the bullets kept me motivated to find their mate. I was exiting the door when a box caught my eye. I lifted the lid thinking it was the perfect place to store a gun. When I looked inside, I felt like I'd hit the lotto. To this day, I don't know if there was a gun inside that box because I never searched it completely. I was distracted by the first thing I saw, stacks of crisp hundred-dollar bills. He could keep his guns; I'd buy my own. I had never seen so much money except on TV, and it was all mine. There were so many hundred-dollar bills that I stopped counting. I started thinking it would take too long. I immediately got nervous like rich people do when they get around poor people. I started packing all our things to leave, I was about to leave but then I realized my mom wasn't there. I was tripping, looking out the windows waiting for her to get back. She was taking too long. I got tired of waiting so I left on my own. I had made it around the corner when I realized I had no idea where I was, or where to go. So I rushed back and waited anxiously for her to get there.

She and Patty finally came back tipsy and laughing about something. When she came into the room we shared I shocked her by being wide awake and fully dressed, with all our things packed. A mother knows her child, and Darlene definitely knew me. She said, "What did you do?" I didn't lie. I hadn't lied to her since the dynamics of our relationship had changed.

I dramatically tossed a fist full of hundred-dollar bills towards her and told her it was hers. I fully explained what happened, and said we had to go. She was heated, she went to see the damage I caused to the door, then went through the motions of saving her son...again.

Gene was not one to be played with. My mother knew my actions put me in danger. I was too unsophisticated to understand. I was deluded, thinking life was an ongoing get rich quick adventure with no consequences. Even in the square's world, it wasn't easy to become successful. It rarely happened overnight, and those who created success often made enemies along the way. There was not a lot of difference in that regard between the working man's world and mine. The main difference was the nature of the responses of the enemies you made. In the streets the police don't get involved until after the response. There is no civil dispute or lawsuit, one person goes to criminal court, while the other goes to the hospital (if they're lucky).

I wasn't fully aware of all the realities of the world I'd chosen because time after time, I had been escaping the consequences of my actions. I thought I was invincible, when the truth is I just caught a few good breaks. The main one was being Darlene Austin's son. After calming down she called a cab to take us to a hotel. I got the best room available for all three of us. The following day we headed to Camden, New

Jersey. We had a memorable layover in Washington DC because I convinced my mom to let me shop for her. I got her a pair of Jordan's, and a MCM sweat suit despite her objections. That wasn't her style. I had never seen my mom in casual clothing. All she wore was heels and diva styled clothing just like Aunt Tilly.

We were going to Camden because my mother was still holding out hope that keeping me from Buffalo would keep me out of the drug game, out of jail, out of an early grave. So, we went to my aunt's house in Jersey. It was actually fun, we were enjoying our Jersey family, who are the best at hospitality. We were spending money like it was raining hundred-dollar bills. I even went to the local bank trying to purchase thousand-dollar notes just to flash them. Once I found out they cost more than they are actually worth I decided against it. Soon life's balancing sheet presented itself. When you cheat to get ahead it never lasts long.

One day I saw this car I wanted that was for sale and I realized I would be broke if I purchased it. So, I dug down in my old bag of tricks. I started looking for a drug connect. I was ready to finally bring my vision to life and start making serious money. It didn't take long; predictably my mother was disappointed. Despite being displeased she didn't chastise me. There was nowhere on this earth she could have dragged me that I was going to be able to leave me or my demons behind. She could prolong it, and cause me to falter for a moment, but try as she may, I was determined to chase down my self-destruction. This was the only road I knew my way down. I found two separate drug connections. One for crack and the other for marijuana. I was told by some guys I met through one of my female cousins that I could make a lot of money with both.

Things were smooth for a short period of time. I had my signature bags of crack, which fittingly had the skull and bones stamp. I was making fast and easy money. Then karma bit me in the butt. What goes around comes around. I've learned this through life's hard lessons many times over since then. However, at fifteen I was the smartest dummy I knew, and life taught me my first major lesson the hard way. I had a team of workers selling for me, all older than I was. The same guys that told me what drugs would sell. They were doing pretty good helping me make serious money. As a reward I took them to a club they wanted to go to. I was never into crowds, so I don't like the party scene; but it's what they wanted. I treated them to whatever they wanted. My age was not an issue to get in the club. No one asked for identification, the money I was flashing was more than enough to gain admission.

Suddenly, my cousin's boyfriend said he didn't feel good, and he left. I had a feeling he was lying, it seemed like it was some sort of stunt. I ignored my instincts thinking there was no way these guys would try anything with me. They had to know there would be consequences if they violated. Hindsight tells me this was likely the same thought that Gene had when he found his room door off the hinges and his money and jewels missing. After about another hour everyone was abruptly ready to leave. Now I felt something was definitely wrong. I went back to my aunt's house, and when I walked in, I asked my cousin where her boyfriend was. She told me he stopped by for a second, then he had to leave.

I raced upstairs to the room where I kept all my drugs; everything was gone. I checked for the money I had stashed in my aunt's safe; it was still there. Thankfully, he was only aware of the drugs kept in that room in a specific spot. Had he looked around, he would have found some other very valuable things. This ruled out the possibility of it being anyone else. There was nothing out of place, it had to be one of the few that knew the exact location of the drugs. My first thoughts were to kill him and his friends. Then a strange thing happened. I started thinking... and this was a first. I was usually a person who only knew how to react, and I typically did that poorly. But this time I had something to lose.

I couldn't recognize the significance of this back then. I wasn't even aware of the change. Prior to that moment, I was living without a care in the world. I knew what I wanted, and I was recklessly chasing it without the slightest care or concern for how I got it. I had nothing to lose, and nothing I cared about. So, thinking about my actions or the consequences of them was a foreign concept. Then I became a bit of an overnight success. I was in the exact position I'd been fantasizing about since I was about nine. This changed my approach. It made my actions matter. Now I had something of value to lose. I decided to take my time, think of the right way to respond. I needed to do it in a manner that wouldn't expose me to the risk of losing everything I was building.

At the time this thought process wasn't clear to me. It's only now that I am able to identify the motivations for my actions back then. In an effort to properly respond I took a trip back to Buffalo. My goal was to visit my Granny Love, who I missed dearly. I also wanted to make a few dollars while there and purchase a gun to take back to Jersey. While back home I linked up with Shady, he immediately saw I was not the same. We were hanging out for a few days when we ended up meeting this family from Chicago that lived across the street from Shady. After this chance encounter we started hanging out with one of the sons of the family named Tone G. He was a notoriously known gang member from the South side of Chicago. They called it the graveyard. I liked him immediately;

he looked exactly like the stereotype of what comes to mind when you think of a gangster. He was light skinned with long hair, and full of charisma. I was in town to have fun, so I decided to treat them to the movies with a few girls. We had a good time, and by the end of the night I'd convinced Shady and Tone to come back to Jersey with me.

This was perfect. Now I had a team to return with. It would be a smooth in and out, then they could go back home without a trace. As soon as we arrived in Jersey my aunt knew I brought a new element with me which screamed trouble. She tried to talk some sense into me. I love and respect her, so I did listen. We decided to chill. My cousin Shady wanted to go out and party and chase behind girls as always. I took him to one of the clubs. It was the weekend, so it was lively that night. Going out was a huge mistake. My cousin was doing a lot of flirting and Tone was just a natural ladies magnet despite his uninterested expression. The locals were clearly jealous. This soon turned into a fight, which led to something bigger.

My plan was out the window. The only part that came to fruition was that they did leave without a trace. The only problem is, I had to leave with them. My uncle got us back to Buffalo just as quick as we came to Jersey. I was told to stay there; my aunt was done with my trouble. I was back home which was not a total disappointment, but it did change things dramatically. I wasn't living a law-abiding life in Jersey, but I was doing better than I would in Buffalo. My quality of life changed in many ways. For one, at least in Jersey in 1993 I didn't need to carry a gun every second of the day. At home I had to carry *and use it*. My mother tried to give it one more chance, it almost worked, but my fate was sealed.

CHAPTER NINE
Friends With a Killer

My first few weeks home, I literally went home. A few years prior, when I left at twelve, I vowed to never return. In defense of my vow, when I returned, I wasn't just living off of my mother or my Granny Love. I was paying my Granny Love money for my own room. The house had four bedrooms and two were vacant, so I rented one of the empty rooms. She didn't ask me to; I insisted so I felt like it was OK, I was back home but like an adult, not a little kid. I wasn't there much anyways. It was more like a trusted storage space. Most days I would be out all-day hustling and getting reestablished. I had just lost an entire functioning operation, so being back to the beginning was like night and day. In Jersey things ran like a legit business. To operate efficiently you had to develop certain business skills like marketing. I had built my own Brand. After successfully doing this your business ran itself if you employed the right people. The customers would come searching for a specific brand. In Jersey they came looking for my skull and bones stamp.

Back in Buffalo there was no organization at all. It was every man for himself. Only the strongest of the tribe would survive. So, I was back to being required to operate with an element of violence or risk being destroyed by my peers. I had no desire to lose and would barter with my life to win. My mind (or what little of it I had at the time) was made up. By any and all means I would reach for the stars. Sadly, in these impoverished communities that's not very high. For us some jewelry, a nice car, a gun and five to ten thousand dollars is considered an achievement. Many lives are sacrificed for even less, and mine happened to be one of them. Each second that passed I was losing more and more of myself.

I was a bit intrigued by the entire family I met from Chicago. They had an obvious sense of unity, loyalty, and love for one another. I started to hang out on Titus Street with them. My cousin Shady lived across from them and would go to clubs with Tone G. I would skip the clubs and stick to chasing money. Shady had a lot of feuds going on due to his underhanded dealings with various women. These issues caused problems everywhere he went. One incident led to Tone G killing a man who wanted to fight my cousin. Tone said that where he was from, there was no fighting; there was no such thing as a "fair one." He told my cousin and his brothers to walk away. He pulled his gun out while also telling the dude that wanted to fight Shady to do the same. Upon realizing that this was not going to be fair, nor would it be a fight, the man took off running up Sycamore Avenue. Tone purposely waited until he was almost a block away and then fired one shot. The shot hit the man in his back, and he died. I was told about the incident, and it didn't scare me away. It actually made me grow an affinity towards him. He was cold, calculating, and demanded respect. Those foolish enough to not give it to him died. There was no middle ground, no compromise. If you were his friend, or family of any kind no one dared to cause you harm, but if by chance someone who hadn't gotten the memo tried it, they felt his wrath. Since I was a pup, I was searching for role models, and he fit the bill. I was immediately in awe of how he carried himself.

Another night out at a club we called "the killer point" due to all the shootings that took place there, my cousin ran into one of his longtime enemies named CJ. Predictably, their feud was over a girl they were both dealing with for years. When CJ saw my cousin, he planned to kill him, and would have if not for Tone. This was no chance encounter. My shady cousin took Tone there knowing they'd likely run into

CJ. He knew for a fact that Tone wouldn't hesitate to kill CJ if he tried to start anything. My cousin feared CJ; many people did. He was a notorious shooter himself who enjoyed killing and intimidating people. So, when my cousin met someone just as ruthless, and even more capable and willing to kill, he came up with a plan. There was no match between the two killers. Tone was born into one of the most infamous gangs in Chicago, the gangster disciples. He was raised in one of Chi-Town's worst neighborhoods. In the midst of it, he became one of his gang's elites. So that night Shady took him to the killer point knowing there was a great chance he would see CJ and Tone was the weapon that he'd use to finally off his enemy. In his mind Tone had recently demonstrated his willingness to kill for little more than perceived disrespect, so this was the perfect plan.

The messed-up part is that Shady never told Tone or anyone else about this particular ongoing feud, or the imminent risk of danger involved with going there. This was a place CJ was known to frequent because it was in his neighborhood, and it was the place to be on a Friday night in 1993. When CJ arrived, he noticed Shady and like clockwork it was on. He approached and there was an immediate exchange of gunfire inside the club. The place had no real security, so there was no stopping it. Surprisingly, despite the hail of gunfire, neither shooter was hit. Both CJ and

Tone got away untouched, however now the feud was intensified. It was no longer a beef between two men about a girl; it was now a blood feud between two killers who didn't even know each other.

After the shooting at the club Shady started avoiding Tone, which didn't go unnoticed. I was with Tone every day, but we could never find Shady. His disappearing acts caused a lot of friction because he was the one who had set this feud aflame, and now he was nowhere to be found. Tone was hunting CJ at all hours of the day and night, and CJ was doing the same. There were shoot outs, and near misses and things continued to escalate. One morning Tone's mom got in between an incident when CJ and his right-hand man B-Boy came looking for Tone on pedal bikes. She was more gangster than all of them. She made CJ tuck his gun and ordered Tone not to kill them right there, and everyone complied. With all this going on Shady was across the street hiding in the house; pretending he was sick, or that his girl wouldn't let him leave. This infuriated Tone, so when he finally caught Shady, he told him how he felt. He said, "I killed for you, and I'm in these streets everyday fighting a beef that I don't know shit about because I fuck with you; but before I let some female come between the bond we got, I will go in that house and blow her brains out."

He had a way with words and how he delivered

them that put an end to any question about his authenticity. Those words scared my cousin. He knew he had bitten off more than he could chew. He promised Tone that he would get up with him and convinced him that things were not as they seemed. But instead of keeping his word, he went to some other guy's house that lived next door to him and lied on Tone. He told these dudes that Tone was planning to kill them. He offered to set Tone up for them. Tone had a reputation. Buffalo wasn't ready for a savage mentality and unshakable resolve like his. He was shocking to everyone, even to those men who themselves were considered dangerous. Compared to what Tone came from, they were elementary. So, with Shady's help, and motivated by fear, they planned to kill Tone. They had no idea everything he told them was a lie. He had his own reasons to want Tone out of the way, which was to save his own life.

A few days passed and Shady started to come around more. Unbeknownst to us, he was only getting close enough to set Tone up. It took him about a week before an opportunity presented itself. Tone came down with some type of bug that knocked him off his feet. Thinking back now, maybe this part was no coincidence. Tone decided he would go to his girlfriend's because only his trusted family and friends knew about her spot. This was my cousin's opportunity. He called the men and took them to the house where Tone was. They decided to ensure that Shady couldn't turn on them and sell them out by making him participate in the shooting. One of the two men did the driving, while the other and Shady did the shooting. They crept onto the porch and approached the front windows. They were able to see through the curtains that Tone was laying on the front couch watching TV. They both fired into the house. Tone could have retreated further to the back of the house to try to get away or to save his life, but he was raised to be a G. That wasn't just a part of his nickname, it was how he lived.

He had a gun beside the couch. While being shot he retrieved his gun and tried to return fire. The heavy incoming fire was too much for him. He was hit. My cousin Shady called me after the shooting and told me all about it. He tried to explain his reasoning and claimed he was scared. Tone had him living in fear. In his mind he did it to save his life. He cried his confession, and his words ripped through me and tore at the strings of what heart I had left. I didn't know Tone for long, but in the few months I knew him, he proved to be a friend. In the hood it's hard to meet people you can trust. People you can count on to always be real and not stab you in the back no matter what. Tone was all of this and more to me. I knew without any doubt he would never be anything but a true friend. He would never turn, never tell, and never fold. With most you could only hope, but with him you knew he was a true friend and a true G.

I got his name tattooed on my right forearm, and I mourn him as a brother. My relationship with Shady was never the same. It was strange after that. I loved him like an older brother. I had looked up to him since I was a little boy. This confused me tremendously. I was at odds with my feelings about him and the situation. I was confused as to where my loyalty should be. I was so embarrassed that my own cousin was responsible that I didn't even attend the funeral of my friend. Ironically, Shady, being the sick and twisted person he was, had the nerve to be sitting in the funeral service like he was mourning the loss of a friend. I think he got some sort of kick out of it. After this I started to focus on my hustle and avoided my cousin as much as possible. I wasn't scared of him; I just didn't trust him. I loved my big cousin, and he was a friend. I was just having trouble processing what he'd done. So, I started dealing with him in small doses. Eventually, I pushed it to the back of my mind, holding on to it as a point of reference regarding his character.

A few months later Shady was arrested for a different case. Even though I didn't trust him and knew he was foul, he was still family. So I held him down. Between me and his girlfriend Angie, we made sure he had everything he needed while he was locked up. We took care of him. Sadly, this good deed wouldn't go unpunished. Shady also had a daughter on the way by another girl and in addition to helping him personally and helping Angie raise his lawyer money, I was also helping the mother of his child that was on the way. At fifteen this was a lot. Things were stressful, but I didn't complain. I did as any true friend should; I held him down. Despite my feelings about his involvement in the murder of Tone, I went hard for Shady. Angie and I did whatever it took to make sure he was good. The two of us bonded as a result. She saw that everyone else had turned their back on him but me. We were oblivious to the whispers of others who were creating rumors about the two of us. We were too focused on helping get Shady home to concern ourselves with anything else.

Someone was telling Shady that the two of us were involved with one another sexually. Instead of confronting either of us to get to the truth, he decided to keep it to himself. After we reached our goal, his lawyer was paid, he got a sweet plea deal, and he was saved from many years in state prison. Once our mission was accomplished, Angie and I fell back from running with each other. Despite the rumors, there was never any sex between us back then, not even a hug. The two of us were so focused on doing what we could to help Shady that sex was the last thing on our minds. Hindsight says that Shady was simply unable to recognize what loyalty looked like because he had none of the identifiable qualities in himself. After giving all I had to help him, I was broke, miserable and out of options to get back on my feet. My mentor was still around but our communication was off and on, more off than on due to my own poor choices. So, my foolish pride prevented me from going to the one person who could have helped me. Another thing that kept me from confiding in my mentor was the fact that when Shady went to jail, he left with some bad blood between him and my mentor, so I felt guilty by association.

Had I swallowed my pride and gone to him he would have happily helped me out. But I knew that his help would have been accompanied by some tough words, and I avoided the truth I knew I'd get from him. Out of desperation, I did one of my own sleazy moves. It was something I had done a few times in the past to get out of a hole. I would take twenty dollars, go to the record store where they sold bottles of a drug cut called comeback. This was only meant as a form of cut for cocaine. I had none, so I cooked the cut with some baking soda the same way I would make crack. I then took the fake drugs to sell. I would usually do this with a few people, then buy real drugs with the proceeds. By the time the people came back complaining I would replace the "mistake" with real drugs. My customers would then see me as a trustworthy person and look to do more business with me.

This was a long way from where I was several months earlier which had me stressed. I would think of Jersey a lot, and of Tone. I was at a very low point, I started to regret a lot of things. Looking back, I'm sure I was clinically depressed the entire time. I was avoiding dealing with the source of my depression. I was the classic victim, blocking out my trauma in order to cope. Unfortunately, in the type of community I was raised in, you're trained to always be okay because help is almost never on the way. You have to be strong, endure, keep going, survive. I didn't stand a chance of being noticed, or properly diagnosed. I was on my own, which meant I was headed for much worse than I'd already experienced. There was no other option available. This is the reality for so many people growing up in poverty-stricken communities, brimming with broken homes and inundated with a variety of untreated trauma. For us, befriending a killer is normal and becoming one is common.

CHAPTER TEN
Running Out of Time

Since my return to Buffalo, it had been one misstep after another. I could not seem to get my feet settled under me. I was constantly on edge, fighting for every inch in life. I was barely making it and completely uncertain in life when an opportunity for change was presented by an unlikely source. I would go to my Granny Love's house at certain times to accept collect calls from Shady. I had a separate phone line put in specifically for this purpose. He'd typically call with various requests for me to connect three-way calls to other people or wanting updates on what was going on in the street.

On this occasion he called with a different agenda. He had met some girls from Bradford, Pennsylvania that were planning to come see him. They needed help locating the jail once they arrived in New York. As always, I agreed to help. He started telling me that one of the guys he was locked up with told him that Bradford was a nice place. He suggested that I could go there to check it out when they came to visit. I told him I would think about it, but I would definitely make sure they got there for the visit. When they arrived, I showed them where the place was, and after the visit my cousin kept insisting that I should go back to Bradford, Pennsylvania with them. I thought about it for a few days and decided there was no harm in checking it out. I had nothing going on in Buffalo, so maybe this would be a new opportunity.

One night two girls came to pick me up. I jumped in their Caravan in search of a fresh start in a new state. I didn't think to tell anyone; I just left. I was hoping I would find something similar to Jersey waiting for me. My mind was focused on getting back at least a taste of the "success" I had in New Jersey. I was excited, and ready for something new. One of the girls who picked me up was named Tisha; to my surprise, she immediately started to come on to me while her friend Reeba drove. I was a bit confused because she was supposedly my cousin's girl. More importantly, my mind wasn't on sex at all. My top priority hadn't been sex ever since I got my hands on all that money in Richmond, Virginia. At that point I was much more enamored by money than any cheap thrill.

Tisha was an attractive, voluptuous woman. I just

had no interest in anything other than regaining the ground I'd lost over the last several months. So, as we drove, she continued to try to physically please me. I didn't stop her; I sat there and went along with it, but my mind was preoccupied. I was in a state of depression that had gone unrecognized. I was obsessed with using money to medicate my deep-rooted pain. We arrived in Bradford after midnight; the small town was dead silent. I couldn't get a good feel for the place in the darkness and quiet of night. We pulled up to what I assumed was their residence. I zipped up and buttoned my pants as we pulled in front. Tisha was visibly disappointed and perhaps feeling insecure because she was unable to make me ejaculate. I had no way of telling her the truth because I didn't fully understand myself at the time. It wasn't even about her. The problem was that I wasn't present in the moment; my mind was immersed in aspirations for money, far removed from sexual pleasure.

Upon entering the house, I could see that it was lively and full of people. They were drinking, dancing to music, and having fun. I could also see that mine was the only black face in the crowd. Everyone else was white with the exception of Tammy's boyfriend who was Mexican. Tammy was another one of their roommates, the rest were just friends there to have a good time. I was instantly comfortable. I didn't feel judged or the need for any kind of defense mechanism. They didn't see me as a threat which is what I was used to around people that looked like me. By that time even relatives looked at me with eyes full of judgment and apprehension. This clean slate was refreshing and comforting. They offered me drinks as well as other party favors. I declined, letting them know I didn't drink or smoke. Now that my anxiety from traveling to the unknown had calmed. I was drained.

Tisha sensed my exhaustion and took me to the bedroom to sleep, but once the door closed, she had other ideas. She was all over me, and this time I went wild. I took my frustrations out on her body. The complete 180-degree difference between my response to her in the van and my eager engagement now made her jump to the conclusion that I just didn't like oral sex. But that was way off base. I loved sex, especially oral sex. The truth was multilayered, but I just had too many thoughts racing through my head on the ride from Buffalo to Bradford to enjoy her hospitality.

A few days passed, and I learned that things were slow in that small town. It was quiet in comparison to the other places I had experienced, and I liked it. Tisha and I became an unofficial item. I just went with the flow. I was searching for an opportunity to reach my goals. I was obsessed with the idea of dealing drugs for money, my medication, my pain reliever. The chance came when I was just about to give up and leave Bradford. A drug addict that lived around the corner came by the house. Tisha warned me not to deal with her because she was a crack addict. Unbeknownst to her, this was the person I had been daydreaming of. This was the only reason I got in the van to come to Bradford in the first place.

I discreetly learned where she lived, and how to find her house and later that day I went to talk to her. I told her I was able to get anything. I asked her what would be the best thing to get and how things worked in that town; what the prices were, where the hot spots were, who were the players. She was like my college professor, and I needed these office hours so I could ace the final exam. She told me how to win without even knowing it. In her mind she was running game. To her, I was a fool she was going to play. Unfortunately, she was unaware of the fact that I was raised by a master game runner. She had no way of knowing that this kid she was coaching with bright brown eyes and a quizzical look, had been born to Darlene. She didn't know who I was, but I had been raised by a woman who had prepared me to see her kind coming from a mile away.

When I left her place, I was ready to execute my mission. I was broke, in a new town, and about an hour and thirty minutes away from home. I was living off the people who had invited me. I felt like a sucka every second of everyday that I wasn't earning money. I had to get home, get some product, and get back to town. After a few days I decided I would get some money from Tisha and contact my mentor. I hadn't been around Coldspring in a minute, so the heat and the "troublemaker" stigma attached to my name in the streets had fizzled out a bit. I was able to make some calls and set up a trip supposably to go home and visit my family. However, when Reeba and Tisha drove me back to Buffalo, the last thing on my mind was family. I went to my Granny Love's house to call my mentor and let him know I was in town. I met up with him and explained what I had been up to and my current situation. He proceeded to tell me the reason I was having problems. I was trying to do too much and be too many things.

He accurately diagnosed my issue. I wasn't satisfied with the money. I also needed the attention, both negative and positive, but my attention seeking conflicted with the goal of making money. Much of what I was doing was a hindrance to ever being successful. He then reminded me of something significant. He asked me if I remembered the time, he asked me to find someone to do a job for him. I immediately recalled the whole scenario.

My mentor came to me and told me a guy owed him money and was making excuses about paying. This same guy had just purchased a new pearl white Mercedes. The car was parked at his mother's house, and my mentor wanted the car firebombed. He told me to have one of my boys do it and he would pay them four ounces of cocaine, or ten thousand cash. When I heard the compensation package, I told him I would do it myself. He was instantly disappointed in me. This was the only time I had ever heard him slightly raise his voice. He said, "I'm trying to teach you how to be a boss.... how to get things done without being on the front lines. The dudes on the front line go to jail or die early, and BROKE! I'm trying to teach you how to do this right, but you keep wanting to be the fool. Never mind, forget I asked you".

I remembered it all. I had never forgotten, and since that day our relationship was strained. That day he embarrassed me. At the time I did not know how to tell him that I had been damaged. I didn't know how to tell him that I felt that all I deserved was being used. I didn't know how to tell him because I really had no idea at the time how to articulate my truth. I believed I was "the man". Yet I lived as if all I was worth was an early grave, or a prison cell. He made his point painfully clear with that walk down memory lane, then he told me to keep the short money I came with and to stop by the house to see him later. I agreed even though I had told my ride we wouldn't be in town long. There was no way I was going back empty handed. So, I told Tisha and Reeba I had to see someone before I could leave. They agreed to wait for me and that night at exactly eight I went to his house. He told me I could get any quantity I wanted to take back. He just wanted me to be smart and stop playing both sides of the game.

I really didn't think I would need that much in such a small town. A ten-dollar bag of crack in Buffalo was worth fifty dollars in Bradford. I did the math and decided to take a quarter ounce of cocaine that I would cook up myself. This was worth more than three thousand dollars in Bradford. I knew I had to go slow or end up in prison. Things got good for me quick. Before long I was back and forth to Buffalo a lot. I was also selling marijuana through a few people who worked for me. The marijuana would be gone as fast as it arrived. In the meantime, Shamel had come home from the Carolina's so I went to see my brother from another mother. I tried to convince him to move to Bradford with me. He stayed about a week before he got homesick, and I had to take him back. On one of these trips my cousin Tim "the tickler" asked to come to Bradford. In my mind I convinced myself that I was past the trauma of what he had done all those years ago. I did my best in my head to make it my fault. I refused to view myself as a victim. Had I allowed myself to admit that I was his victim, I would have killed him. Instead, I took the blame from him and placed it and the shame on myself. This allowed me to protect the secret. It was a classic case of victim self-shaming. So, when he asked me to come, I agreed. I engaged in Olympic level mental gymnastics to suppress my feelings about him and how uneasy and creepy I felt whenever he was around.

Predictably, these feelings eventually resurfaced when he started being around me in Bradford, especially if there was any threat of the possibility that we would be alone together. I would avoid that by all means. The excuses for it varied in my head. I didn't know how to process my feelings. So, I mostly ignored them and avoided him. After a while, it was apparent that he planned to stay. He and Reeba hit it off and he was going to move in with her. At this point, I knew it was time for me to relocate. It wouldn't be easy. I didn't know many people in town other than the people I came there with, and the rest of my connections were for business. There were a few other women I knew but nothing stable.

One day two people I kept hearing about, but had never met, came by the house. One was a white girl with dirty blonde hair and clear blue eyes. She was about 5'6 in height and 145lbs. Her name was Jennifer. She was with a guy that everyone called her pimp. He was a little midnight black man, about 5'2 in height. His name was Little Dave. I could immediately tell they were very different than most of the people I had grown accustomed to in Bradford. This got my attention. I had been told that he sent her to Canada to prostitute for him. I was curious to know if he did this to support a drug habit. The word was that he used to smoke, but now he was clean. I had to see for myself if that was true. The two moved into a studio apartment on Main Street which, true to its name, was the main attraction in that small town. On the weekends, teenagers, as well as adults would hang out on Main Street. Those who had cars would ride back and forth on Main. They called it "flaming the main". People would flame the main until the wee hours of the morning playing music. Others would be on foot doing the same. This was where all the excitement in town took place; where most of the bars that people hung out at were located.

Jennifer and little Dave lived on the strip. I started hanging out with little Dave at their house. Jennifer had three of her four kids living with them. I preferred being over there because I could escape the weird feelings I was having at Reeba's with Tim being around. I started doing my business over on Main Street, and the business grew. Little Dave knew everyone. He started to make me money through other sources. I would pay him for his help. I expanded to surrounding towns, some back in New York state. I was selling weight to dealers in these towns. One day I had to meet with someone on the New York side of the business. I told Dave to ride with me. He didn't want to go because he had a warrant in New York. I talked him into riding with me because it was just an in and out trip. As providence would have it, after I made my drop off, we got pulled over for no reason. The police zeroed in on Dave. They ran a warrant check and arrested him on the spot. My driver, a Dominican buddy of mine, and I were let go.

Randomly getting pulled over like that was suspicious to me. Someone had to call the cops to report Dave. I tried to bail him out which was impossible. So, I made sure he had everything he needed while in custody. I took Jennifer to visit him often. I hated going inside the jail, but I went in once, never stopping to realize that this was the reality I was spending day and night chasing. I was moving too fast to notice the signs around me. There would be plenty of time to read them later. I had to get money, which was all that mattered. No price seemed too high back then. Business was still smooth and getting better by the day.

Jennifer's girlfriend was having a party, and she was tired of sitting around the house, so she asked me to go with her. By this time Dave had been in jail for over a month. I really didn't want to go because I didn't feel like dealing with her friend's boyfriend. He would always screw his face up whenever I was around. He seemed to have a problem with me because he preferred being the only black guy around. It was comical. I had no idea that he was also dealing with two women behind his girlfriend's back that were also dealing with me. But at the end of the day, I didn't care what his issue was, so I decided to go with her. I was still staying with Jennifer after Dave went to jail. She wouldn't take my money for rent, so I felt the least I could do was go with her.

The party was at a small apartment and people were packed inside like a can of sardines. Everyone was dancing. I didn't know anyone else, so I danced with Jennifer. I figured it was better than some random dude dancing with her. In full transparency, I didn't know how to dance. This was not my scene. In the past when I went to a party, I was the one holding up a wall. I was never comfortable enough to dance. A girl could come and dance on me as I stood against the wall, but that's about it. That night Jennifer talked me into just having fun. At one point she took me to the kitchen. She grabbed a drink and told me to try it. I said, "You know I don't drink." She said, "Me neither. This isn't liquor, it's a wine cooler. Just taste it." She coaxed me into it. It tasted like a peach drink. We danced some more, and between sips of wine cooler, and dancing there was kissing. My head was spinning, I was buzzed. I was also feeling a bit of betrayal. This wasn't right, but we didn't stop.

We went home and had the wildest sex all night long. We were out of our heads. When it was over, there was no turning back. The next few weeks things continued. She still went to see Dave with me encouraging her. She took a trip to Canada to make some money like she used to do with Dave. I tried to discourage her. I told her she didn't have to do it. She insisted on pulling her own weight. We tried to maintain the boundaries of our status as friends, but things escalated between us. The transformation of our relationship and the true nature of her feelings for me became clear when I brought a few guys into town from Buffalo.

I had met my boy Terrell through my cousin Shady while they were in jail together. I used to make three way calls for Terrell while he was locked up. When he came home, I tried to help him get on his feet. I invited him to Bradford and had a bunch of girls at the house and we were all having fun. There was one Spanish girl there who was tipsy, and really freaky. Terrell's cousin Jackie came with him to Bradford, and he took the Spanish girl in a room. I went to the room they were in just to see what was going on and Jennifer came busting in. She started flipping like she was my girlfriend, and I was in there trying to do something with the Spanish girl. In truth, I had been sneaking around and hiding what I was doing with other women as if I actually thought she was my girl too.

It had been weeks since we took a trip to see Dave. I had even stopped trying to talk her into going.

Our one-night indiscretion had morphed into this unspoken and unexpected relationship. There were no more trips to Canada. As my birthday approached, we learned that we had the same birthday. She was turning twenty-four, and unknown to her, I was going to be sixteen. She thought I was turning nineteen. We started to settle into a sort of family life, things were natural, and going good. Then without fail, something went wrong. It always did, and this time was no exception.

The first customer I ever had in Bradford got arrested. She didn't know I was aware of her arrest, but I kept tabs on everyone linked to me in that town. She was busted coming across state lines buying crack. I had strict rules which even the local police respected. I ran my operation like a legitimate business. I was finally following my mentor's advice. There were no complaints against me from anyone. There were no reports of suspicious traffic at the house. We lived above a local bar and there was another one right across the street. Both bars closed at 2:00 a.m. So, I had it set up so that the traffic to and from my business blended in with the bar traffic. I closed faithfully at midnight, so all my activities were covered by the environment's natural camouflage. Closing early upset some, but most understood.

I had no control over a few fools like this one who'd gotten arrested in the middle of the night coming from Olean New York. She made a deal with the cops to set me up, but I had been trained by the best. I was more than two steps ahead of her plan. I knew how to spot and spin things like this. When she came to my house the morning after her arrest, I observed that she had way too much money. She never had that kind of cash. This coupled with her being released from jail so soon was more than enough warning on its own without the inside information I already had. But no matter what, because of her, now my spot was hot. I had to do more than just turn her away. So, I told her an elaborate tale knowing she was wearing a wire. I told her my drug supplier had cut me off. He told me I was too hot, so I didn't have any product. She begged me to help her get anything. I decided to provide her with some false intelligence. I told her I would get dressed and take her to ask him to deal with her directly.

I had her follow me most of the way, then told her to wait at the corner. I then went to a nearby house where one of Jennifer's friends lived with her boyfriend. I pretended to have a conversation with him, and then returned and told her that he said, "No." She was persistent; she gave me the money and told me to get it for her. I pretended to go make the deal for her and then returned. I handed her a zip lock that she thought came from him. When she left, I knew my time was up; I had to shut down. That night a local police car was parked in front of the apartment. Jennifer took her innocent all American looking self over to the cops and asked why they were there. The cop told her there was a report of drug trafficking coming from the apartment and they were told to watch the location until a search warrant could be served and executed. We packed up the kids and were in a U-Haul on our way to Buffalo by the next day. When the warrant was served, they searched both places. The one I had led the girl to, as well as the apartment on Main that we fled.

CHAPTER ELEVEN
You Can Run But You Can't Hide

I was back in Buffalo, and this time I wasn't alone. I had a ready-made family; a woman with three kids, ages eight, four, and two. My luck seemed to be holding strong so far. My mother happened to have a nice two-bedroom apartment she recently rented. She was trying to use it as an incentive for me to come back to Buffalo. She wasn't comfortable with me being in Bradford alone. So, when I found myself needing a place, once again she came through. The place was newly renovated, and she was hardly ever there. It was like perfect timing. She hadn't yet made it home, so she cleared her personal belongings out and we moved in. We put the two oldest boys in a room together with their bunk beds. We kept the baby girl in the master bedroom with us in her bed. The transition for the kids was smooth, which was most important; but this abrupt move, and loss of income was costly. It didn't take long for money to get tight.

The bills started rolling in, and so did the pressure.

I reached out to my mentor to update him. My move back to Buffalo was not welcomed news. His advice was that I fall back and take it easy. In his opinion I shouldn't return to the neighborhood at all. In his view I had already demonstrated that I didn't know how to act around my friends. With this option removed, I had to figure something else out. After a few weeks of pinching pennies, Jennifer came up with an idea I didn't like at all. She suggested that she go over to Canada for a weekend to make some quick money like she used to. Despite my protest, she was determined, and she convinced me that it would be OK. She said she could easily make a minimum of fifteen hundred, probably closer to two thousand. This would take care of the bills and give me some room to re-establish my hustle. I would regret letting her talk me into it because this was the beginning of the fall of my house of cards.

Jennifer assured me that she would take a friend so I would feel better. She took a girl named Becky with her. This girl was a rookie. She had no experience and no business ever being out working with Jennifer. The same night they got there they both were arrested. Since Jennifer was known in the area, she was held in Canada. Becky was sent back across the border with a warning. Now I was broke, Jennifer was in jail in another country, and I had three kids to take care of.

I had no idea how long she would be in custody. The only thing I knew for sure was that I would not turn my back on her or the kids. I had to figure out how to survive. Through this experience I got a little taste of what it's like to be a single parent. It ain't easy. I tip my hat to single parents for the daily sacrifices they make. I didn't do the job justice, but I did my best.

The streets were not an option this time. I was responsible for tending to these kids' needs. I had to cook, clean, structure their day, and do the baby girl's hair. If I got caught up in the streets, they'd have no one, and I couldn't risk them losing both of us; so I struggled instead. Thank God Ma Duke would help out by coming to get the baby girl almost every day. Sometimes she'd keep her for a few days. I missed my little lady, but I was relieved at the same time. I'm sure parents can relate. As Jennifer and I waited "for the Queen to return", as the guards would say to their detainees in Canada, I was taking her calls, being supportive, and being a guardian of her three children. But my immaturity would still show up from time to time.

I made choices that were life changing. The most noteworthy was inviting a girl I had met about a year prior over to the house. The kids were gone; Ma Duke had the baby girl as usual, and the boys were with my mother. This girl named Nicole had strict parents. At the time she was only fifteen. The window of opportunity opened for us to see each other, and we both jumped through it. As soon as she got there, we had a quickie that probably lasted two minutes. From this chance encounter we produced our daughter. After this encounter I decided it had been a few weeks, the Queen had not released Jennifer, and I needed some help. The pressure was getting to me. I was stressed out running out of things I knew how to cook. So, I went to the house of one of my old flings who I knew was a good person that would help me.

When I got there, she opened the door with no shoes on. I snatched her off her doorstep, no shoes and all. In her mind she was just having fun with an old flame and would be right back. Instead, I kept her with me for about eight days to help out. I was just desperate to survive. By this time, I had abandoned my pride. I had pawned my jewelry, and even my stereo system to feed the kids. I don't know how I managed it. I can only praise God for sending helpers my way. Jennifer got out after about thirty days. It was one of the happier days of my young life. I vowed to never again allow her to be at risk of being separated from her kids. This was one of the few promises I was able to keep.

Things were rocky when she got home. I had done a poor job of hiding certain things from the kids. Although they never saw me doing anything inappropriate, just having a friend over cooking for them was more than enough to cause friction. She was rightfully upset. I was feeling worthless because I was still broke. The boys should have been enrolled in school, but Jennifer went to jail, and I was a sixteen-year-old Black boy with no legal claim to those kids. There's no way I could just show up as a kid, trying to enroll someone else's kids in school. They probably would've taken the kids. So, this was another issue. Something had to give and fast.

One night Shamel and my friend Lil Jason were at the house. They were smoking marijuana and for the first time, I decided to try it. This was a big mistake. I got high off a few puffs. I told them let's go get some more. We got in a cab to go to the drug house to get more. Shamel and Lil Jason didn't know my plan. They couldn't tell that I was tripping off whatever we just smoked. A girl opened the door to serve us the marijuana and when she did, I pulled out my gun, and forced everyone to go in the house. I told the girl to give me everything they had. There was another girl inside the house who looked like she was ready to give birth any day. I thought she was crazy for being in a place like this in her condition, but who was I to judge. I had to be at least just as crazy as she was (probably more). Here I was forcing my way in a house that was pitch black except for the light coming from the TV. There could have been someone inside waiting with a gun. I didn't know anything about this house or the people inside. At the time I had a death wish, but I didn't realize it until it was too late.

We left there with a box of marijuana and some money. My boys were telling me I was tripping. Unphased, I told them I had the munchies, so we had the cab take us to a pizza spot. I ordered some pizza, wings, and a few other things. I went out to the cab to wait when something caught my eye. I saw a yellow Cadillac with an older man and a young girl inside. It was about one in the morning, so it was obvious to me what was going on. I approached the car, and I robbed him too. I was straight tripping. I didn't have many inhibitions, but what little I did have dissipated under the influence of what I had smoked. I was free to release all my anger and frustrations on whomever crossed my path. After the car sped away Shamel and Lil Jason were ready to leave. I told them I had to get my food. I took my gun back out and went to get my food free of charge, with a tip.

After that night was over, I never smoked again. I don't remember it, but Jennifer told me I flipped out on Shamel and Lil Jason when we got back to the house. She told me she didn't like how I was acting after smoking. She didn't believe it was just marijuana. But the drug was still just an excuse for me to act out my anger and frustrations. Before I ever smoked that stuff, I was already high on the fast pace and the general chaos and kinetic energy of my life.

Nothing has ever made me more out of my mind or gotten me higher than my life itself. But I was at my limit, and quickly unraveling.

One day I came home, and Jennifer was gone. The kids and all their things were gone. She left without a word or warning. I guess it was self-preservation. Together we were drowning, and I was the dead weight taking us under. She had to save herself, and the children. This also gave me the ability to get my feet back under me. I did try to find her at first, but the guy who helped her sneak off refused to betray her trust. Jennifer knew how to manipulate certain men. She'd batted her eyes a few times at the old white guy who was our neighbor, and he came running to the aide of the damsel in distress. I later learned that he had been helping her for a while to find her own place (which he also paid for).

With Jennifer and the kids gone, I started to hustle again with my cousin Snapper and his right-hand man Monet. I came around when things were shaky and unpredictable. Mo had just shot this woman in her groin area, and she hemorrhaged to death. He was paranoid and trusted no one. He felt it was just a matter of time before someone told, and he was arrested. I did my best to calm him and help him dispose of the evidence. We took a road trip to my old stomping grounds in Bradford. We used the trip as an opportunity to get rid of the evidence. We stayed there for a few days, considering the possibility of setting up shop, then went back to Buffalo. The set up they had was a great one, it just needed some order. I knew how to bring order to the business. There are only two ways; you create and maintain order with finesse, or by force.

I could tell that their particular set up was past the point of fixing with finesse. Sadly, I had forgotten the wise words of my mentor. I ran full speed ahead to the front line of the operation with brute force. I was the Johnny come lately of the crew. Snapper and Monet had already allowed a lackadaisical tone to be established and everyone was used to their laissez-faire attitude. They had no desire for change, no interest in structure, order, or consequences. I instantly became the bad guy, and contrary to what they may have thought, I liked it. I fed off of it knowing I must have been doing something right.

There were countless calculated things I did to make everyone label me "crazy". That was my comfort zone. I was a monster at manipulating my audience. I made them believe I would kill over a dollar, literally one dollar...four quarters, ten dimes or twenty nickels. I made them believe it, and to prove that their fears were not misplaced, I was prepared to do it. This gave me a temporary edge, and led to my inevitable downfall. Without any professional training I had mastered method acting, and eventually I got lost in the character.

I was completely immersed in the beast I became to play my role, and I knew that only death could tame it. I began to cry for death to take me. Not with tears, I had learned not to waste physical energy on tears. Instead, I would build and destroy relationships. I would terrorize people without much provocation. Like a vampire, I fed off the blood, and misery of others. My daily routine of chasing financial gain was no longer enough. To quell my deep-rooted pain, I was the personification of "Hurt people, hurt people." I inflicted pain on others. It could be as simple as being insensitive to someone that cared about me, or robbing a garage full of people at an illegal chop shop (knowing they couldn't involve the cops). I was screaming for death; daring anyone and everyone to put me out of my misery. But the louder I screamed the more it seemed that no one could hear me.

So, I grew even bolder. In my own mind I was invincible. No one stopped me or seemed to be able to. At least not the people I yearned for. Here is the thing, in essence I was running from my reality. Although I was playing the role of a fearless thug, by definition I was being a coward. I had assumed the role of a tough guy to avoid my truth. It was easier hiding behind a character than dealing with how I felt. I couldn't cope with the demons of my past; I didn't have the words or the will. Had I taken my mask off, I probably would have taken my own life. Since I was about twelve years old, I had been screaming "kill me" at the top of my lungs, but the truth is that no matter how loud I screamed for death, I really wanted to live. I now know that my actions that exhibited an affinity for self-destruction were born out of a deep desire for a different kind of life, not a genuine craving for a common kind of death.

One night I was walking, unsure of where I was heading. I did it sometimes to clear my head and be close to my mother. When I was a child, she always took me walking. I ran into my boy Terrell whom I hadn't seen in a while. The last time I saw him it almost landed me in prison for murder. So, we had a bit to catch up on. We talked for about a half hour, and when I was leaving, he asked if I was headed to Jennifer's house. I was confused and asked why he would think that. He told me he'd seen her moving into a house around the corner a while back. He told me some old white guy moved her things in. I knew it was true. He then admitted to stopping by one night and trying to get with her, but she wasn't having it. I told him I hadn't seen her, and that I didn't know where she lived. He gave me the address and a description of the house. I immediately went over there, but she wasn't home. The house was pitch black; I broke in. I looked around and planned to wait on her to get home. She never came. I would stop by every day to check if she was there. A few days passed and I started making myself at home when I stopped by. When she finally came home, she could tell that she had been found and that I had been there. She didn't run off again. She was waiting on me the next time I came by. She told me why she left like that and we went back and forth. She had found out my real age, and she started to see that I wasn't the nice guy she had met in Bradford. I had more edge and darkness than she had ever experienced. This spoke volumes, given that her last two relationships were with pimps.

Despite all the warning signs, Jennifer couldn't see the red flags either. Things went back to normal for us. We were like a nuclear weapon when mixed. Things quickly turned ugly because I was even worse than when she left. I was an animal when it came to my hustle. The guy she used to know was chill, this new version was obsessed. I couldn't be in Buffalo the person she had met in Bradford. Here, I had to be a savage. I would be gone for days, she was used to me being home, and having regular business hours. It was my intent and goal to create structure and discipline, I just could not get out of my own way. I was out robbing drug dealers, and anyone I caught slipping. I had no boundaries, no one was off limits. I would help people get on their feet, rob them, then help them again. I was sick in the head.

One day I stopped by the house just to drop off some money. I didn't fully trust Jennifer after she ran off, so I was hiding my money in different spots around the house. I had already been hiding my drugs in the attic of the apartment when I started going inside the house while she wasn't home. I was planning to leave again right after stashing the money, but before I got the chance to leave, I heard Jennifer start yelling. She wanted to know who the attractive girl was in the car I had parked outside. The girl in the car was just a customer. The white Z-24 I was driving was hers. She would often let me drive her car and I was in the process of trying to buy it from her. I tried to explain everything to Jennifer; I told her it was just business, but she didn't believe me. She said, "If you leave with her, don't come back! Take all your stuff with you now!" I told her I didn't have enough room to take everything that was mine. I then followed that up with an off the cuff and extremely obnoxious comment. I said with the confidence of a cocky man-child, "Everything in here belongs to me... including your ass! Now shut up, I'll be back later!" With that, I left thinking I had set her straight. Even I couldn't have anticipated how incredibly wrong I was. As I look back now, I think some of my crazy and chaos had started to influence Jennifer because she pulled a me on me.

When I left, she burned the house down. Our

apartment and the one downstairs from us went up in flames along with all my money, drugs, and personal belongings. She had taken her clothes and her kids' things to the laundromat and left the rest to burn. I later learned that one of my close family members actually helped her try to make it look like an accident, but the investigators still ruled it suspicious and made her agree to take a lie detector test. She was able to convince some to give her the benefit of the doubt, but I knew in my gut she had done it on purpose. All my things were gone, my savings, my stash, everything. This was a loss I couldn't have anticipated; it felt incalculable. All I was sure of was that the streets would now have to pay more so I could recoup my losses. I passed the bill on to them just like retail stores do to their customers when profits are lost due to increased taxes or theft.

I refused to starve while others ate steak. In my mind you had to eat to live. By natural law, if I didn't eat, I'd die, and I wasn't about to die hungry and alone. So, I fed on those that were doing better than me. It may sound unbelievable to you, but Jennifer and I stayed together. How could I fault her for doing something outrageous when that was my middle name at the time, especially after all we'd been through together? I forbade Jennifer from associating with my cousin who had helped her with the fire. I didn't care what they said or how many times they insisted that it was an accident; I knew I was right about that house fire.

Eventually, months later, my suspicions were confirmed. One day while Jennifer was gone, I checked the mail and found a letter from my cousin written to Jennifer. I guess she was sending letters in the mail because I had barred any other contact. When I opened the letter, all the details of how it went down were inside. Inexplicably, this appealed to my sick way of thinking back then. I felt that with the letter in my possession, I now had leverage that I could use in the future to my advantage. The shocking part is that she had passed the lie detector test, so without the letter, I never would have known for sure. I guess in the end she was more like me than I ever knew. It seems that she too had learned to play a role, the innocent all American girl next door. She was so committed to her character that she was able to force her mind and her body to create the physiological indicators that demonstrate truth, when all the while, it was a lie.

We stayed in a hotel for a few weeks and then we found a new place on the west side. I had been getting busy in the streets, so I had the money we needed for new furniture and appliances. I'm not going to lie; I even got my own man for his stash. Monet had left about three thousand dollars' worth of drugs in the glove box of one of his cars. Desperate times call for desperate measures; I needed that. My back was against the wall. I was like an animal pursuing and feeding on every creature in the jungle. Anybody could get it, even my own kind. There was no rehab on earth for the addiction I had. Drug addicts describe their addiction as having a monkey on their back. Taking a page from their book, I would have to say that I had three silver back gorillas on mine; each pulling me in a different direction with divergent agendas.

CHAPTER TWELVE
The Truth Shall Set You Free

My addiction, which in essence was hiding from my pain, took me to some of the earth's darkest depths. It was the catalyst for some of the worst kinds of evil inflicted by my own hands. Money was just a tool I used to purchase fake love. Some people cut themselves to avoid or escape their true pain; back then my crimes were akin to self-inflicted wounds designed to distract me from my own pain by imposing it on others. This is the cycle I was trapped in. I only speak the truth now to destroy the lies that have hidden in plain sight for far too long. Please don't get lost in the disfunction of my youth. I do not offer this truth for judgment or to glorify violence. My aim is to deter children like me from following my path, to give a voice to their pain, and an insight into the mind of a young man who became a menace.

know first-hand that this kind of conduct is most often an unheard cry for help. Children like me don't cry in the conventional manner, our tear ducts have long since dried up. Out of desperation, we create masks to hide and instead of sobbing with tears, we cry by wreaking havoc and becoming terror. Despite our delinquent behavior, please don't lose sight of our humanity. I will forever be remorseful for all my sins. As one can imagine there are many more examples of my deviant behaviors, but I will end with my most notorious. Not that I am proud of them; I simply owe those who were most affected the truth (which is different than what was portrayed in the media and in court by those who manipulated and misstated the facts to create their own narrative). There is no DNA or crime scene recreation that can capture the hearts of those like me. You must walk in my shoes if you are to judge me right. If not, you will always get it wrong.

It was December of 1994 and Christmas was a few weeks away. I was peaking in my trade as a drug dealer. I finally started to figure things out. I had a child on the way. Nicole was six months pregnant. My thinking was changing. I was also being encouraged by Nicole's parents. They had no faith that two naïve and immature teenagers could parent a child; It was obvious to them that I was a street kid. Her father spoke to me personally trying to get my head on straight. I made all sorts of empty promises when I first learned that Nicole was pregnant. I promised to get out the streets and become reliable long-term. Although her parents didn't believe me, they reluctantly allowed us to keep our baby.

With a few months left before the baby arrived, I assessed my progress. I provided financial support, and I came running each time I was needed, or wanted. I started thinking of more than just myself. All of a sudden, I had a reason to live, and I wanted to. I realized all the lives in the balance of my poor choices. These thoughts made me apprehensive, and I lost my edge. Previously, I was able to convince myself and others that I had nothing to lose, that death would be a welcomed escape. This was no longer true. My mask was slipping. I had a precious life on the way. I felt alive again, and full of hope. I became more aware of what I had rather than what I was missing. I was fortunate to be a homeowner at sixteen, and to have three cars. I had money I hadn't even counted yet and Jennifer and I were about to move to the suburbs. These things used to be my focus, but with my baby on the way, they didn't mean as much as they had just six months earlier.

I started looking for my exit strategy, I wanted out. I was done with my madman act. I just didn't know how to close the curtain and exit the stage. My character and reputation had become bigger than their creator. They took on a life of their own. There was no way they would allow me to walk away or take an early retirement. My character was familiar with the laws of physics; two opposing minds could not occupy the same space. One of us had to die so the other could live. I was trying to resurrect the humanity in me. I wanted the part of me that desired to be a hero when I was six to stand victorious when I was sixteen, but the beast simply refused to die. It had already done and said things that I couldn't take back. The bell had been rung. There was no way to change the consequences or call back the waves of sound that were reverberating throughout Buffalo. My poor choices as a broken child had set my stage and I had cast all supporting roles to other fools just like me. So, there I was wanting to take a bow, but the streets of Buffalo were screaming for an encore, and this is how it played out.

On December 14, 1994, Jennifer and I were preparing for Christmas. The night was festive, and the kids were asleep, so we were sneaking their gifts out of the trunks of the cars to wrap. She had been encouraging me to slow down, but I was in the streets around the clock getting money for Christmas and our impending move. That night I told her I wasn't going anywhere until after the holidays. She was happy to hear it. What she didn't know was that I had plans to transition to something legitimate in the new year. I just needed to figure out what that would look like for us financially. We had options, she was almost done with college. We already discussed her going back to finish. I planned to go back to school, and work with my father. I just needed to repair our strained relationship. I was hopeful for the future. Little did I know that others were planning a future for me too, and their plans did not include a happily ever after.

A guy named Ice had just come home from prison and he was dating one of my cousins. He was with another guy named Tommy (my friend Terrell's brother), and they were planning a robbery. The plan was to rob the house of a known drug dealer. This particular drug dealer's brother and Ice had been involved in a previous altercation of some sort, so this was supposed to be the "get back". While watching the house for the perfect opportunity, Ice noticed my cousin Monique go inside the targeted house. This is when Ice came up with the plan to involve me. Ice was dating my cousin Monique's little sister and he wanted her out of the house so she couldn't identify him. He decided to come to my house to ask me to get her out of harm's way.

At the time, I was staying at 104 Landon Street. The house they planned to rob was across the street and a few doors down. When he knocked on my door and explained his plans, I refused to help. My only advice was to wait until my cousin left. While speaking to him I noticed the people waiting on him in a parked car. It was dark, but I recognized Tommy.

I didn't know much about Ice's reputation, but I knew Tommy. He was a hot head and wouldn't hesitate to shoot someone over the least bit of provocation. Once back in my house his involvement in the plan started to trouble me. I guess I still had a little bit of a hero complex where family was concerned. Despite Jennifer's objection, I got my gun (as I never left home without it) and I went outside. I told them I was going to get my cousin out of that house. I knew in my heart if I had not gone to get her, she would be hurt just to send me a message or to make a point. I knew the way people like Tommy thought; I was one of them.

As I was making it clear to them that I was only going to get my cousin and that would be the extent of my involvement, my cousin Snapper and my partner Monet pulled up. They all knew each other well. They all started talking about what was being planned and now my cousin Snapper and Monet wanted a piece of the action. This changed the dynamics of the situation because of my loyalties to them. In my heart I was done with this life, but this circumstance called for me to remain in character. I was living life as two people at once and even the bible tells us that "A double minded man is unstable in all his ways."

I made it clear again that I would go get my cousin out before they went in. My plan was to walk her across the street to her mom's house and be done with the whole thing. I had no intentions of being involved in the robbery plot, but Monique changed all my silly plans. She came to the door with nothing but attitude, "What you doing here? What you mean leave? I ain't going nowhere!" While we argued at the door, the rest of the guys rushed inside the house. They clearly had guns out but instead of just leaving with me, she ran back inside the house behind them with no fear. I can only guess that because of my reputation, she assumed that I had some influence over them (even though they were adults).

The reality is I had none. I could easily have become a victim in this situation if I made the wrong move. I followed her inside still trying to get her to leave. Things escalated quickly. I was straddling the fence, on the one hand trying not to be involved, but on the other making the most of my mask. I was protecting my persona so as not to become a victim in this robbery that was swiftly going off script. I understandably looked to the occupants of the home like a co-conspirator. I teetered and tottered back and forth from one role to another the entire time which made it appear to them that I was the man in charge.

As I write this, I have no fear of any further prosecution, and no remaining appeals. I've been in custody since January 5, 1995. I have no incentive to lie. My sole purpose that night when I broke my promise and left home was to protect my cousin. She was one of my favorite cousins. I did not want her blood on my hands. Sadly, my decision to save her lead to me being buried alive. I played both sides in that house that night, but I was no angel, and I did more than enough to appear as guilty as the rest. I will not allow history to be rewritten by my own bias. No, I was not there to rob the house, but when someone looked up at me to remember my face, yes, I shot him in his hand.

The robbers soon learned that there was no money in the house. They thought the dealer kept his money there, but he and his wife had split up and he had moved out. The robbery script was now obsolete, so they started to improv. They decided to kidnap his son for ransom. My cousin Monique grabbed onto the son holding him tight. She refused to let him go. She was on the verge of being shot. She had already been given liberties she wouldn't otherwise have received if I wasn't there. But now she was overestimating my involvement, everyone was on edge, all fuses were short, and this was about to end badly for us all. I did my best to diffuse the situation by stepping between the gunmen and her. I told her. "I'll make sure he's okay, but you have to let him go." She reluctantly listened, and I walked out with him. As we walked ahead of the other men, I whispered to him that I had nothing to do with this. This was the truth, although I am sure he didn't believe me.

He and I knew each other for as long as we could

remember. He was a friend. I had lived in his home. His mom was like my own. This was all wrong and I wanted him to know I was not behind this. I can see how my words likely fell on deaf ears as I was taking him from his home at one o'clock in the morning. The facts were much more complicated than they appeared. It was like a weird convergence of coincidences that resulted in a dangerous cocktail of crime, danger, survival, violence, and fear. Some feel I could have let him go right then. Others say we could have run off together. They may be right, but I promise you it's easier to think clearly and logically when you're not caught up in the whirlwind of the situation. And it's even easier to judge from the outside looking in.

On the inside of it, and underneath my mask, I was scared. My whole family lived on that street. The door to my own house (where they knew I lived) was still open and Jennifer and the kids were inside. My cousin Monique was still in danger. There were no evident options available that a sixteen-year-old kid could come up with in sixty seconds. Eventually, after the robbers were far enough away from my home and my family, I did try to get my friend away from them. I snuck to the trunk of the car he was being held in. I got him out and tried to start the car to leave. Because the heat was on while the car was turned off, the battery had stalled. I got caught trying to start the car to take him home. I was desperately trying to escape with him and got caught. This fact was never mentioned at my trial. The district attorney decided to bury it. I don't know how guilty I was in kidnapping my friend; all I know for sure is I also made efforts that night to save him. I would like to think I played a role in him getting home without a scratch.

Exactly seven days later I was hiding out at a girl named Nyree's house due to the heat from the kidnapping. I was trying to figure out how to get out of the mess I was mixed up in. I wanted to get back to the peace I was feeling before those fools knocked on my door. I was stressed, and the reason I was at Nyree's house is that no one knew how to reach me there. Her address was unknown, most (including Jennifer) didn't even know she existed. My only connection to the outside world was my pager, and I was not returning anyone's calls.

That morning I was dead sleep. I had been up for days on edge. Sleep finally won, and I was out. Nyree kept trying to wake me up telling me someone was paging me nonstop. After several attempts she succeeded, and I called the unknown number. It was my cousin Shady, fresh home from jail, my cousin Snapper and Monet. They were all on Landon Street and Jennifer would not let them in the house. They asked me to come over that way, it was urgent. I was avoiding that area, so I wasn't interested. They asked where I was which I wasn't going to reveal, so I gave in and agreed to go over to Landon Street. Instead of using a known car, I called a cab. When I arrived, they told me they called this guy we all used to purchase product from. They used my code when they paged him to get him to bring them some drugs. They told me their plan was to rob him for drugs and money, and then make him take them to his stash. I was pissed and wanted no part in this mess, especially at my house (the same place all the drama from a week before had started). I knew when we decided to stay in that house in my old neighborhood it was a mistake.

I had rules against people knowing where I lived. Especially when people I wanted to protect lived there. Not following my own rules was costing me on every level. The person I used to be who was comfortable wearing the mask would never think twice. He would have been down for whatever. But I was no longer him, my heart had changed, but no one else had gotten the memo, including the fool in me. This ongoing metamorphosis caused me to hesitate, it stole my edge. Without complete commitment to my character, it was inevitable that I would make mistakes. All these lessons wouldn't start to resonate until I was years removed from freedom.

When I had time to look back with a clear head and a mature mind, I understood that I had become a leader with my edge, indifference, and aggression.

There was no one that would dare try to lead me while I was fully committed to my character and sticking to the script. But who was I, and who'd follow me without it? Although I was only sixteen and far from being a man, I had bullied my way into manhood on my own terms. In a twisted way, when I began to reconnect with my humanity, it made me unfit for life in the jungle. In my transition, I became a follower. I could have easily taken control of this situation if I was fully committed to my character, or to my newfound hope. Being stuck in the middle made me ill-equipped to exercise control, and it worked against me in the end.

The man was on his way with the drugs which I could have easily paid for. I could have just given the drugs to my cousins and Monet. What no one knew is that I had re-gained all my lost ground since the fire. The petty drugs he was coming with wasn't worth anything compared to what I was about to lose. Had I been thinking like my mentor, like a true leader, like a boss, I would have paid him (and them) to go away. Instead, I was trying to serve two mindsets with a divided heart. The ruler of my actions and the strongest part of me was still the character I had created to survive. The me I aspired to be was still on training wheels while my character was ready for the tour de France. When I wore the mask, I was heartless. I didn't value life, least of all my own.

Attempting to balance these two beings living

inside myself was exhausting. I just wanted it all to stop, so I made a choice. As the dealer pulled up, I fully embraced my monster. I told everybody there that I was playing for keeps; it was all or nothing. They knew exactly what I meant; this man was about to die. At that time, I was depressed, scared, paranoid about the incident the week before, tired of the consistent chaos of my life and generally unhinged. The world was spinning and had been since I was six. I needed it to stop and this would be the day it did. I would do something that I knew I couldn't come back from, something that would bring it all to an end, something to stop the deafening noise and the dizzying momentum of my descent. To me this was my way out. This would be my final act of defiance. I wanted to leave an unshakable impression that would discourage them all from ever calling on or conjuring Lil Dee again.

To my cousin Snapper's credit, having seen me keep my promises in the past, he knew it wasn't a game, so he left. As the man entered the house Snapper was leaving. They spoke, and Snapper left knowing it would be the last time he saw him alive. I could never understand why he thought this exonerated him from any culpability; he was the one who made the call to get the man there. It was his plan as much as it was anyone else's. Whether he left or not, blood was still on his hands.

Monet greeted the man and told him I was in the kitchen. Shady was hiding in the bathroom while Jennifer and the kids were in the bedroom. The kids were sleeping as Jennifer pretended to sleep as well. When he entered the kitchen, I shot him in both legs. Shady and Monet approached as I demanded the location of his stash house. He kept saying the address, but I couldn't understand him, so I shot him again. When I look back, I was clinically insane. I kept thinking someone had to die so I could finally live. The reality was the monster inside of me is what needed to die. I had shaped and formed this thing out of pain and fear. I created this monster so that I could become what people feared.

I got lost in all the pain of past abuse and instability that had charted my course to become this. No one knew that since the age of six I'd fed on this evil and created my own. Many have asked who else shot this man, and who else played certain roles. Here is the truth; others shot him too and played a major role in his death. However, just as in the kidnapping case, I never revealed those details to the authorities, and I was the only one charged with both of these crimes. I am the only one doing time so I will leave their details to be told by them. I own my actions and I've paid and continue to pay for them, as I should.

I know that the payment of my debt to society for what I've done will never be enough for his loved ones. As I stated when my family lost Steve, a killer has no idea how many lives are in the balance. "Sorry" is simply never enough. It does absolutely nothing to fill the void. So, while I am sincerely remorseful for my abhorrent actions, I won't waste my time or theirs with how sorry I am. I believe that the best way for me to atone for the harm that I've caused and the trauma that I've inflicted on others, is to use my story to help prevent confused, damaged, or misguided, youngsters from walking my path.

Many people suffered from my behavior on both sides. My pain going undetected, and my inability to cope in a healthy way was the catalyst. I took the easy way out, the way of a coward. I want to encourage others to be better, and to be brave. When you see a kid lashing out and acting as if they don't care, it's likely that you're looking at another me. There is no doubt the kid is hurting and probably scared. Try to uncover and acknowledge their pain and implement a healing process instead of writing them off and watching from the sidelines as they destroy themselves. How we as a society and as a community choose to deal with young people's pain matters. So if you care to judge, dare to save.

CHAPTER THIRTEEN
Welcome Back to Buffalo

After the shooting, things got even more out of control. I went on the run (in reality I had been running since I was twelve; I just failed to connect the dots). Jennifer left town before I did. She took the kids back to Pennsylvania with her parents. I left a few days later, it was the day before Christmas. I headed back to Bradford to meet Jennifer and get her settled with the kids. Then I planned to go to Seabrook, New Hampshire where I had a friend that no one knew about. None of my plans fell into place. Jennifer never met me in Bradford. I didn't know where she was, and I was worried that something was wrong. I went chasing behind her to be sure they were good. I should have worried about myself. I wasn't thinking straight. I was off balance when it came to my self-preservation. As a result, I was arrested shortly after finding Jenifer and while in route back to Bradford.

Six days after my arrest I was being driven back

to Buffalo by two homicide detectives. Once they got me back, I was arrested for kidnapping in the first degree. I was told I would soon be charged with murder. I had destroyed the life and future of the boy in me who wanted to be a fireman. My motive was hatred. I hated what I thought I had allowed to happen to me. I hated what I allowed my response to be. So, I destroyed my life. As much as I had hurt others, it was lost on the arresting officer and the judicial system how much I had also hurt myself. After my arrest and arraignment there were a million revelations all at once. The first epiphany was who my true family and friends were; the list was shockingly small. The people who showed up were mostly those I least expected (people who could have easily treated me the way I had treated them).

My first visit was from this girl named Sonya. She was a young girl I was dealing with; by young I mean my age. In comparison to the grown women in my life, she was a baby. Not old enough to be coming to a visiting room alone. You had to be eighteen or older to visit without a parent. Imagine that; you can't visit a jail alone at the age of sixteen, but you can be detained in one. She had used someone else's identification. The peculiar part about it was that no one knew I was in custody besides my mom and Jennifer. So, getting a visit from Sonya seemed impossible. I walked right by her to sit at an empty table thinking she was there to visit someone else. When I realized she was there to see me I asked her the obvious. Apparently, she'd been worried about me because she hadn't heard from me. She'd been calling the jail with my name daily. As soon as I arrived, she knew. She said that she put a letter in the mail and immediately came for a visit. This was significant because it showed me what genuine care and concern looked like. It also gave me a stick by which to measure others, and most didn't measure up. I quickly learned that they couldn't be bothered and couldn't care less.

The list of disappointments was plentiful. Some of them had actually done their part to ensure that I was there with their deceitful slithering tongues. I had invested in and built the foundations of my persona on fear. But when people know you're facing life in prison with no way out, that fear fades quickly. Shortly after word of my arrest got out, my house was robbed. Angie sent me pictures from a family get together and I saw some of my family members wearing my clothes. These were custom made items that no one else had. Now I knew who had robbed my house. It was my own family, which tore at my heart. I was just on the front line for these people. Soon after that the letters from Angie started slowing up. I later learned that my cousin Shady had beaten her up badly. He accused her of having sex with me while he was in jail. He forced her to stop writing me and took the money she had to help with my legal defense. The revelation of who was who became clearer and clearer each day. My life literally seemed to change overnight; and the truth is that it did. But the change had happened years ago. The day that evil man touched me my life changed.

Nyree came to see me; she made sure I had underclothes. She told me not to worry, she would stand by me through this even though I had lied about my age. The following week she was in my face in tears. My own family and my so-called friend told her lies about me. They told her I had robbed her house. They even told her that I had HIV, and she should leave me alone. Then while she was upset, they tried to come on to her. It was Snapper and Monet, my partners. Nyree was an extremely beautiful woman, so I understood the urge, but to me nothing was worth that kind of betrayal. I was crushed, and despite our valiant efforts, our relationship could not survive those attacks. The list of betrayals continued to grow and destroy my spirit. Karma kept coming to mind, I was getting back what I had earned. I shouldn't have been surprised, but I was, and it hurt. The only hope I had was the one bright spot I managed to create, which was my unborn child. She was all I had in the end.

The money, the fake friends, and most of my family were all gone. The one sure joy I had was the child that I had betrayed the most. There I sat in prison, with charges that could get me twenty-five years to life, and other charges yet to be filed that I could result in fifty more years to life. I was so caught up that I had lost sight of what was true. I kept it real with the streets. I refused to talk for the streets. I was about to do a whole lot of time for the streets. Now I was realizing that I had left an innocent child in the streets, without her father. God only knew how that would turn out.

Pretty soon it was time for trial. Things had fizzled out and the case went cold on the impending homicide charges, so my only case was the kidnapping. I was thinking, that although the truth of how things went down that night sounded crazy, it was still the truth. So, I thought I had a chance if the truth came out. I learned that in our system, justice and truth are not synonymous, and never guaranteed. Oftentimes, in our criminal justice system the truth is secondary unless you're a part of a certain protected class. In my case, I was a street kid that had made horrible choices to put myself in this position.

No one told the truth, at least not the one I knew. A cohesive storyline was created that the jury could follow. This story made me look nothing but guilty. I was a fool to think it would be otherwise. There I was telling my side sprinkled with a mixture of lies and omissions. I was making sure I didn't implicate anyone else because my priority was not being a snitch. I looked like an idiot that no one could believe. In an effort to protect other people, my testimony was that I didn't know the men that kidnapped my friend, and they didn't know me. No one could believe my version of events. What I was trying to sell was ridiculous. I was lying too much and trying to be too loyal to the streets. The lies that wove into my testimony made it impossible for the jury to see the parts that were true. That loyalty cost me a lot; it always does.

I was found guilty as charged on all counts with the exception of the possession of a weapon charge. I was headed to state prison for a long time, possibly the rest of my life. I had lived all of sixteen years and here I was about to spend my best years in a cage. I could cry but deep down I knew I had chased down this fate. Regardless of what I said, and despite some of the mitigating circumstances, I deserved to be in this position; I had earned it. On the thirty-first day of January 1996, I was sentenced to eighteen years to life in prison. After the guilty verdict the prosecutor held a press conference vowing to make sure I never got out. They were committed to making sure I did life. I was a teenage lifer, there was no way out. I went back to my cell that night not knowing what year it would be when I went to the parole board to beg for a second chance. All I knew for sure was that I had been a fool. I started to think of how I got there.

I retraced all my steps and took notes of my travels. I asked myself was it worth it; I needed no answer. My heart was clear. I failed myself and I knew it. Despite whatever had been done to me, I had failed myself. I could blame whoever I chose to if it would help me sleep at night. At the end of my list of excuses I had to face the fact that while others had also dropped the ball, I failed to show up for myself. I allowed what was done to me to be an excuse, when it should have been my reminder of how not to treat myself and my motivation to treat others well. God saw fit to allow me to encounter deep hurt and pain at an early age. I had a duty to make sure I used it as a reference. Instead, I used it as a crutch and an excuse to fail. In my heart I knew I had hurt so many people and this was the consequence.

Somewhere I had a man's family mourning his loss. I had Nicole's mother crying for what her daughter was facing trying to raise our child alone. I had Nicole crying, not knowing what she would tell our daughter when she wanted her daddy. There was no taking anything back. I knew my road was long, and my lessons would continue to be learned the hard way. I found myself alone. At that time I didn't believe in God, so I didn't even have a faith to fall back on or find solace in. I balled myself up, threw the cover over my head and tried to cry. No tears would come.

I had forgotten how to cry. I don't know, maybe I was in character and didn't care. Maybe I was in a state of shock. I fought for and against sleep as I had since I was a child. I wanted to sleep but I was afraid to go. I was at my worst now and sadly; I was in a place where no one cared. If I thought I had gone unnoticed before, I hadn't seen anything yet.

A few days passed; my mask was still in place. There was no need to remove it now, in fact I was going to need it more than ever. I held on for dear life and braced myself for the unknown. I was going to be shipped off to a prison in the mountains of New York, but before I left, I wanted a visit. I didn't know when someone would come to see me up in the mountains. I called my young trooper, Sonya. Despite the odds she had been a main stay. Everyone else had done a disappearing act. As I was on the phone planning our visit for the next night, the guard called my name. I told her to hold on so I could go see what he wanted. The next thing I heard was the guard saying, "Pack up, you're going off property to state prison." My heart dropped and my mask fell to the floor. I responded in protest, "I just got sentenced. It should be a few days before I get shipped out. It's the middle of the night."

My words meant nothing. I was state property and they had come to collect. The thirteen months I was in the county jail I had been a handful. I had multiple assaults on staff and had one pending felony assault on a sergeant. I had done much more than the average adolescent. They wanted me out of their facility and tonight was as good a night as any. Just as quickly as Buffalo had welcomed its native son back, it had prosecuted me, sentenced me, and sent me packing. Now it was time to say goodbye. I got back on the phone to say goodbye and then gave all my things away that I couldn't take with me. I stooped down to the floor to pick up my mask and put it back on with the fake smile attached. Then I left. I had been a fool many times before, but never in the face of this. Under my mask I was scared; terrified really. I feared I'd never get another chance at life.

CHAPTER FOURTEEN
A Kid in The Big House

The following morning before sunrise I was escorted by van to state prison. I had never seen them take someone to state prison this way. Usually, a bus load of people would leave together. They would go to Wende Correctional facility first to be processed in the state system, then sent to Elmira the following day unless it was a weekend or a holiday. I was in a van by myself and was told my destination was Elmira. The trip was long, lonely, and nerve wracking. I felt like I was leaving the country instead of driving just three hours away. When the van pulled up in front of Elmira Correctional Facility it was worse than I imagined. It looked like an old mediaeval castle with a dungeon; the type of place where you could go in and never come out.

We went through the front entrance which I later learned was also unusual. I had to walk past an old statue of two naked boys. The inscription said something like, "you come in a boy, and leave out a man, only the strong survive." If I was nervous before, I was terrified now. I hadn't even seen the inside of the place yet, and I already felt myself being reformed. Being processed into the prison was degrading. I was stripped of much more than my clothes and dignity. They stripped me of my name. In some clerical mix up my alias was listed as my real name. Despite my protest that my real name is Derrel Moore with one L. The guards insisted my name was Derrell Austin. I was ignored and told my new name. I had never spelled my first name that way, nor had I ever officially used the Austin last name. Now I was told this was my name as long as I was state property. So now, in addition to my prison number, I also had to learn a new name given to me by the prison guards at Elmira. I was coming into the big house with absolutely nothing, not even my name.

For the sake of seeming very strong and extraordinary I wish I could say I was unmoved; that I got inside and was the toughest guy on the cell block. Then the other more compassionate side wishes, for the sake of those I hurt, I could say I was caused some extreme harm. Maybe that might ease the pain of those that I caused pain to. But the reality is my fears were actually worse than what was awaiting me. In fact, most of the hardships I eventually encountered in prison were all self-inflicted. As always, I was my own worst enemy and it would take some growing up before that would change.

If growth, transformation, or restoration was the goal, prison was the worst possible place to be for a kid with my issues. On the other hand, if the goal was purely retribution, it was the most appropriate place for me given my crimes. Under New York State law sixteen-year-olds are recognized as adults in criminal court. I couldn't buy a drink from a liquor store, and even in state custody I wasn't old enough to buy cigarettes from commissary. I could get a life sentence at sixteen, but I couldn't get a square until I was eighteen. I learned pretty fast that most prison rules were counterintuitive and nonsensical. In fact, the main rule in prison seemed to be that the rules and policies were prohibited from making sense.

We could purchase all the canned goods we wanted from commissary (which could easily be turned into weapons), but if we allowed our fingernails to grow too long, we'd get a misbehavior report, and more restrictive confinement (because our fingernails could be used as weapons). So let me get this straight, buy all the sharp can tops you want that can slash and cut human flesh to the white meat, just don't grow your nails long enough to scratch someone. This was my new home. I had a rough start because I couldn't adjust. More than two decades have passed since I have been here, and I still struggle with it. So at seventeen it was impossible. I spent close to six months in a reception unit, waiting to be classified and sent to my first permanent prison placement. When I was finally designated, I was sent to the adolescent capital. A place called Coxsackie Correctional Facility. I had heard about this place; it had a reputation for being full of New York's wildest youthful offenders. It was six hours from Buffalo. I didn't really care how far from home it was or how wild the prison population was reported to be, what scared me or turned me off from giving it a chance was the fact that the facility didn't have a trailer visit program. Other facilities had trailer visit programs that allowed inmates to spend a few days alone with family or with their wives if they were married. If I stayed at Coxsackie, I wouldn't get any trailer visits.

My new reality was that I was going to be in prison for a long time. I had no interest in being confined in a facility possibly for life with no trailer visit program. I wasn't even going to try. So, the first day when I was out for the morning breakfast run to the mess hall, I cut myself. I told the prison staff I didn't know who did it. The staff didn't believe me, and I didn't care. They could put me in segregation or protective custody. It did not matter, I just wanted them to get me out of there, which they did. The irony is my efforts to get moved out of Coxsackie were diminishing my chances of getting a trailer visit wherever I ended up. I was having too many behavioral problems. I was always in trouble, and the first prerequisite for getting a trailer visit no matter where you're housed is staying out of trouble. I hadn't thought things through.

I was eventually assigned to a facility program called, "custodial maintenance". The instructor was trying to teach me how to properly sweep and mop. The law library was right next door to where I was supposed to be learning how to mop, which presented a problem for my future success in the maintenance program. I had just started a life sentence and while I wasn't the smartest idiot in the facility, I had enough sense to know that I was in the wrong room. So, I'd consistently get caught in the law library when I was supposed to be learning how to use a mop ringer. It sounds funny now, but at seventeen with a one-year-old daughter and faced with spending the rest of my life in prison, I didn't get the joke. Every time I got caught, I'd get put on lock down. I'd do my time, and they would send me right back to the program.

In my heart, I felt it was against my nature to sit there accepting my fate without fighting. I couldn't live with myself if I just sat there learning how to use cold water to mop. I had to at least try to go next door to find out about my constitutional rights and how they were violated at trial. So, I would go and get locked down again, but I refused to break. Lockdown meant nothing to me in comparison to what I was using as my motivation, my beautiful one year old daughter that I needed to get home to. Eventually, when it was clear that I wasn't going to stop, they assigned me to a new program away from the law library. Had I been a bit smarter, and a little less angry at the world, I could have recognized that my approach was counterproductive.

At the time I had no vision. I couldn't see clearly or comprehend what was best for me long term. Afterall, I was in prison in part because of my short sightedness. If I could go back and tell that fool anything at all, I would warn him that he is his own worst enemy. I would caution him to slow down and listen. Unfortunately, we often learn as we live, so many of life's discoveries are the result of us doing it (life) wrong. In my case I had done so much horribly wrong, and I wasn't done yet; in fact, I was far from it.

After a few birthdays passed by in the big house, I'd experienced a failed marriage to Jennifer at eighteen. It lasted about as long as some of those two-week celebrity marriages that end up being breaking news on TMZ. People made pit stops in my life as if I were a 24-hour gas station. So, my heart grew colder with each agonizing disappointment. Throughout it all there was one constant who never let time nor distance come between our friendship. In those years Angie was my ever-present north star. Choosing to be a faithful friend to me cost her dearly. She suffered insults and countless physical assaults from my own cousin who couldn't stand that she was loyal to me, and refused to believe that we were just friends. Even now she remains my friend and I can count her and God as my most unlikely main stays during those dark days.

I must clarify that I was raised to believe in God, but somewhere along the way I lost my faith. Then the more self-hatred I displayed, the less I believed and the guiltier I felt. Then it got so bad that I was dead inside and I concluded that there was no God. When I found myself alone, yearning to pray and desperate to believe, my knees wouldn't bend. I was ashamed and afraid that I had done way too much wrong to be accepted by a God who is always right. I simply avoided all thoughts of God. I was certain that I'd spend the rest of my life in a cage without Him. I felt like I was at war with the world and even with God. Then when I was at my worst, I knew beyond all doubt that it was God alone who was there. His remarkable, and incomparable Mercy was lifesaving.

God sent mercy after mercy in countless ways, and through countless people. I live without doubt that it was The Most High that sent people to stay for a season or two in my life. There were periods when I was getting four to five letters a day from Angie. Her words inspired, encouraged, and helped my growth. She owed me nothing, this was God working through her which I am sure she would confirm. As the people I loved most did things that caused me pain or worked to break my resolve, it was this balance that kept me at bay. I would get all the way up to the edge and stick one foot over the side of the cliff, and God would send someone my way to give me hope and pull me back from the brink. In those days I teetered on a tightrope between hopelessness and hope. God's mercy is how I held on.

At one of those times I was feeling defeated, Nickie, the girl I was crazy over as a boy dropped in my life out of nowhere. Her letter had the power to resurrect me from my depression. We had never said more than five words to each other, but here she was sending me a three-page letter that put a battery in my back. It made me feel like I was still alive, and still mattered. She showed me that my life wasn't over, and people still cared. We exchanged letters, promises, hopes, and dreams, and in no time, we were planning for marriage. She was about to turn twenty-one, and I was about to turn twenty. We were just two young kids in love, but prison was an old beast in control. We never stood a chance, and I didn't make it easy. Due to my adjustment issues and defiant behavior in the facility, I was constantly placed in solitary confinement and moved from place to place. I was sent to a brand-new prison called Upstate Correctional Facility in the mountains of New York state which was supposed to be a facility specifically for New York's most troubled prison population. I was on one of the first buses to be sent there in July of 1999. We were an experiment. Upon our arrival the facility had no medical staff and there was no law library. It had opened before it was fully prepared to house inmates.

When I got my first visit there from Nickie, she was shaken by the sight of me behind the caged gate which is how that facility conducted visits. It was literally like visiting a zoo. It was too much for her. She refused to kiss me through a gate like all the other visitors did with their loved ones. She also made sure to let me know that she wouldn't be back to see me there like an animal. I did time there in what was considered the most extreme form of solitary confinement and then I was moved to Sing Sing Correctional Facility. After being in such a restrictive environment, everyone thought I should be happy to be transferred to Sing Sing, but all I could think about was how far away it was from home. I kept thinking, "No one will visit me now."

When I got there, I was allowed to make an arrival phone call. I didn't even want to tell Nickie where I was. I just called to tell her not to worry about where I was because I wouldn't be there long; I had a plan. It worked before so I figured I would do it again. She insisted that I tell her where I was and stop acting crazy. So, I told her, all the while bracing myself for rejection because I was too far away, and this prison stuff was too much. Her response astounded me. She simply said, "I'll be there on my day off," and she was. I felt like "the man". But I continued to get in trouble and made no effort to behave so I could get closer to home. I turned Sing Sing into my personal playground. I was making money in there just like I was in the street. I had cash money like it was legal and no fear of being caught due to the many officers who were complicit. In the meantime, I had no idea that my selfishness was destroying my relationship.

I thought things were great until Nickie didn't show up for our prison wedding. I was crushed, and it was even worse when I found out that same week that one of my appeals was denied. Devastated, I went off the deep end for a while. I had my mask on tight. I was back to not caring about anything. I became the leader of the notorious gangster disciples in New York State prison. We were acting a fool in Sing Sing. I didn't care and I made sure all my recruits didn't either. After the wedding "no show" Nickie was still hanging around, but the handwriting was on the wall.

One particular time she came to visit, and my mask was nearly cemented on my face. When I got down to the visitation room, I planned to prove I did not need her. I told her to go to the bathroom where a girl would be waiting to tell her something. What she didn't know was that there was another inmate who owed me money, and the plan was for him to give it to his girlfriend at the visit so she could pass it to mine in the bathroom. When she came back to our table, she gave me a reality check that helped me grow up a bit. She refused to be a part of my plan. She wouldn't take the money from the girl. She told me I was a fool; still in prison being the same idiot that got me there in the first place. She told me how she was working sixteen hours a day just to be able to come see me, take care of her kids, and pay bills. All I had to do was stay out of trouble, so I could move closer to home. She felt that she was the only one making sacrifices in our relationship. The least I could do was stay out of trouble so I could move closer and make it easier on her. Instead, there I was still being a criminal and trying to get her to do the same by taking drug money in a prison bathroom.

She was right, and had I been ready to receive that heavy dose of reality I would have stopped. But I didn't. I wasn't ready. I kept going, and as a result it would be more than four years before I saw Nickie again. I didn't know it at the time, but her blistering rebuke that day was more than just a "get your shit together speech" it was a goodbye. The truth is a part of me had been waiting for her to leave. In my cynical mind, everyone left, and she was no exception. At least, this way I could tell myself that she didn't leave me, it was me that pushed her away.

When Nickie exited my life, I retreated even further into my shell. I was moved by her words and her withdrawal from my life, but I buried the pain. I had a life sentence that I'd probably die doing. If I couldn't see her anymore, so what! I hadn't changed at all. If anything, I'd gotten worse. Now I was angrier. I created a new, much longer list of other people to blame for my mess. I was good at blaming people for how I treated myself. After about two years the unthinkable happened. I got kicked off of my own playground. I was so incorrigible that I actually got evicted from Sing Sing. When they put me out, I was sick. I felt like I got arrested all over again. In Sing Sing I didn't feel confined. I was living like I was free. I ate what I wanted, did what I wanted and had more money in my mattress than many people had in the streets. When I was there, I had fun although I was doing life.

Many have told stories about Sing Sing and some of those stories have a lot of truths in them. Then there are some fools who, unsatisfied with their own narratives, adopt and misappropriate other people's stories. But I was Lil Dee, and I made my own. I'm sure someone somewhere is telling my story. Don't worry, I won't blow your spot; carry on soldier.

CHAPTER FIFTEEN
She Promised to Always Be There

When my mother was diagnosed with lymphoma in 2002, I was devastated. She finally started to enjoy her life despite my situation. My incarceration had been hard on her. I am sure she blamed herself and there was nothing I could say to stop her. My mother had gone through every level of drug addiction from dealing to using. My own troubles only made it worse; fueling her need to numb herself. Drugs were the crutch she used to deal with her demons. When her only child was doing a life sentence, her addiction escalated. So, when she moved to Atlanta and started pursuing her music dream, I was happy for her. She would send me pictures of herself performing all over the country. She even opened for Lenny Williams, which was one of the happiest nights of her musical life.

She had a music label called M.L.I. records, "music, life, intelligence." She put out her own original music while in talks with major labels for distribution. And just as she gained momentum cancer came calling. It was time to pay for all she had done to abuse the temple God gave her. Her diagnosis broke me. Especially when the doctors told her she had only months to live. I didn't know how to deal with it. I shut down and blocked it out. Then her hospital stays became more frequent, and her weight started to drop.

God had my full attention. For the first time I begged, bargained, and pleaded. In spite of the doctor's prognosis, months turned into years. We had scare after scare, but she'd always pull through. My mother was a fighter. Cancer was no match for that crazy lady. There were way too many things we still had to work out between us; things that needed saying. We both made our fair share of mistakes that hurt. We needed our moment, but we kept putting it off believing God would give us tomorrow. Almost five years after she was diagnosed, she was admitted back into the hospital. Even in her condition she was still calling shots. She was able to pull the right string to arrange a deathbed visit for me to come see her from prison. My pain was so great that I was numb. It was like a state of shock. She was my lady, the one I could always count on when I needed someone. The truth was, she was the reason I could pretend not to care about anything or anyone. She was my safety net, and I could do anything in this life as long as she was in it.

When I got to the hospital, I expected to see her hooked up to a bunch of tubes and unable to speak. But that wasn't Darlene. She was a woman who often did the unexpected and through sheer will accomplished the impossible. When I walked in her room, she was sitting up in the bed with the most beautiful smile you'd ever want to see beaming on her face. She had the kind of smile people would pay to see, and that day she had it on full display for me free of charge. I had no way of knowing it was all an act, and she was in unbearable pain. I guess my mother had a mean mask game too. She had always been there for me when I needed her. So in her mind, that day would be no different, no matter what it cost her.

There were no signs of a dying or defeated woman. All we had was an hour per prison rules, but we laughed, we joked, and we loved on each other the whole time. She tried to feed me but all I wanted to do was look at her. I had to be sure she was okay, and this was not goodbye. She assured me it wasn't. She told me she would see me again soon. She even pulled out a fist full of money, and said it was for me. She asked if I could take it or have someone come pick it up. I agreed to have someone come to pick it up. I wasn't worried about money. I was just glad she was okay. I left happy to have seen her, and she seemed fine. I was content for the moment. That feeling only lasted long enough for me to be escorted to the elevator in the hospital hallway. As I approached the elevators with my escorting officers, my mother suddenly began screaming my name. She always had the loudest voice on the planet, and she used it that day. "Dee! Dee! Dee!" I got this strange feeling as she screamed my name over and over that her wailing was our goodbye. Her beautiful voice yelling my name is forever imprinted in my mind; those were the last words I ever heard from her.

My mother died on August 26, 2005, right around the time of hurricane Katrina. One half of me died with her. The death of a parent is anticipated. It's the natural order of life. Sadly, I had not lived a natural life. I never anticipated her not being here. I didn't know what I was supposed to do without her. Life simply made no sense with her gone. I didn't know what message God was sending me. God knows my heart. My heart was Darlene, so why would he take her knowing I couldn't live without her?

It was all very hard to comprehend. Without her I was certain I was on borrowed time. With the consistent care and concern of my father, a friend of mine named Jasmine, and Nickie (who had recently re-entered my life) I was able to limp along day by day and barely get by. God used each of them to keep me off the edge of life's cliff. I had someone, sometimes all of them, visiting me every day. I was only twenty minutes from home at the time in Wende Correctional Facility. God had placed me there; believe me I didn't get placed there for good behavior. It was a mercy that likely saved my life. I needed constant human contact so I could have something to hold on to other than desperation and despair.

A few weeks after her death I had a trailer visit scheduled. It was perfect timing, I needed to get out of prison because I was dying inside. This visit provided that outlet. When I got out there, I was finally able to cry. I had been holding my tears back for more than eleven years. Inside that trailer I cried for all my losses, but most of all, I cried for my regrets. I had been a handful. I required way too much from her and had given way too little in return. I wanted a do over. I needed a second chance at being her son. I wanted to listen, be a good boy, go to school, and make my mommy proud. All the things that I had spent years spitting on, I wanted them back. I knew I would never get a do over. Life is not something you get to screw up then do over when you finally feel inspired. No matter how badly we need or want it, there simply is no do over; but there's always an opportunity to do different.

I got lost for a few months in my own self-created drama with the women in my life. At the time it served as a good distraction. When Nickie came back into my life out of nowhere, I was already dealing with another woman named Jasmine. I met Jasmine through one of my sisters over the phone while Nickie and I weren't speaking. We connected intellectually, and when she asked why I had the name Nickie tattooed on my ring finger I told her our history. So, it was no surprise to Jasmine when Nickie popped back up. Both women would race each other every morning to see who could get to Wende to see me first. They would both sit in my face waiting for me to choose one or the other.

This drama provided a temporary amusement to take my mind off of the extreme pain caused by losing my mother, but once again the burdens of life brought me back to reality. Unexpectedly, my Granny Love's health took a turn for the worse. Before I knew it, I was back in the same hospital, on the same floor I was on nine months earlier with my mom. As I was escorted past the door of the room I had visited my mother in, it took all my willpower not to run in there to see if she was still sitting in that bed with her beautiful smile. My knees felt weak as I passed by, and I still regret not being able to check and see for myself.

When I got to my Granny Love's room, I could see she was in bad shape. My uncle Robert, and my grandfather were by her side. When I walked in Robert left to give me time with her. My grandfather wouldn't leave his wife's side, it was apparent to everyone that he was in agony. He just needed to be her rock and be there to help her understand who I was. At first, she thought I was my mother. She missed her loudmouth child, and it showed in the way she called me by my mother's name. Then she realized it was me and tried to get up out the bed from her excitement. She told me she had to listen to the doctors' orders so she could get out of there and get home to me. She thought her grand baby was free. I didn't have the heart to tell her the truth. She was crying tears of joy, and frustration at the same time. In her mind, her baby was free, but now she was the one confined. I took this time to say all the words she needed to hear in order to let go in peace; words I needed to say in order to do the same.

As I've said before, the law of physics can never be denied. Two opposing ideals cannot live peacefully in one mind. One has to die so the other can live in peace. It was time for me to live in peace, but first I had to destroy the beast, and that beast was my excuses. That day I told my Granny Love the truth. "Granny Love, none of it is your fault. You did the very best you could. You were a great mom, as well as a great Granny Love to me. You did not fail us; our actions are not your fault".

I continued by thanking her for loving me even when I didn't deserve it, and I told her that I loved her. My words eased the distress she'd been holding on to for so long. She asked for reassurance of the truth in them, and I promised her that she had been amazing. I told her she had done a great job and could rest knowing she was a great woman. She then struggled to ask me a question, then followed it with sound advice that I will cherish forever. When I was done, I knew I had told her the truth and most of all I knew it was time I started to own it, all of it; my poor choices, my destructive behaviors, and the hurt that I had caused to so many.

She thanked me for my words, and unlike the visit with my mother, I knew this was goodbye. I left in tears. This time I didn't hide them. I wore them proudly. I knew I would never see this sweet loving woman again; not unless I started paying back what I owed. She had no doubt earned her way into heaven. If I ever wanted to see my Granny Love again, I had some serious work to do. When I got back to the prison a peace came over me. The two pillars of my life were gone, but the real me was back. It was time to put my big boy pants on and take my mask off. I could do one of two things; grow up and live the life I was created for, or fold. It was time to prove how tough I really was. I had shown that I could be a coward and take life. Now it was time to prove I could give life, and I had to start with myself.

My mother had broken a promise she never had

the power to keep. The lesson was clear, there is only one certainty in life (and death) which is God. We all live according to God's will. We can waste our days doing nothing, going nowhere, and making excuses, or eradicate the excuses and live. I chose to live. I did not bury my Granny Love or my mother. They live on in my heart. What I buried was my demons. I was done being a victim of others, and especially a victim of myself. The tortured boy in me could only be vindicated by the man I was capable of becoming. So, I chose to rebuild myself. I chose to live regardless of where on earth my physical body happened to be. When all the dust settled it turns out that Darlene was true to her word. She is still here, living through me, smiling through me, and protecting me.

CHAPTER SIXTEEN
Devastation Inspired Change

When I was at my lowest and up against the worst enemy I ever had, with all the excuses I needed to quit, I found the fortitude to move forward and became reacquainted with my humanity. I had used every excuse I could my entire life in order to rationalize my awful behavior. With the two most important women in my life deceased and Nickie whom I loved, cheating on me again, I had more than enough excuses available. My normal pattern would have been to use those excuses to sanitize my scandalous behavior. Breaking the pattern would prove difficult. I had regressions as well as doubts, but I pressed forward, determined to grow up. As Nickie's visits became less frequent and that familiar look in her eyes became more vacant, I refused to fold. I pretended not to see it, but I couldn't pretend not to care.

I started to understand that hurt people find

ways to hurt other people, often unconsciously. She was a woman rooted in pain. I was able to recognize it because so was I. We eventually split again, and predictably, after a few months she resurfaced with another child. As much as I loved her, I knew the two of us could never be (not that we didn't try again, and again). I say this and pray that all those that matter will understand. I thank God for all the lessons which ultimately turned out to be blessings. While I regret my actions, I have no regrets about my consequences or the lessons I've learned as a result of them, and I hold no hard feelings.

One can reasonably conclude that each person incarcerated has a laundry list full of reasons why they're there. When you combine the most common factors leading to incarceration with the losses many of us have taken along the way (like my childhood trauma that went unaddressed) you have a perfect recipe for a tragic conclusion. If not for the mighty protection and mercy of God I would be completely broken. I would still be living in my tragedy proudly. I understand that this may sound absurd, but I dare anyone to walk half a mile in my shoes without ending up the same (or worse). It is only by God's grace and unsearchable will that I still exist.

I was fashioned by God's hand to take each step on my path and preserved to come out the other side to call attention to and be a voice for the lost. I beg you to get involved as a parent, a relative, even a friend or advocate. I wanted more for my life, I needed more, and as God has proven to me, I deserved more. It wasn't until I lost everything, I thought I could never live without, that I recognized my worth. There is simply no way we can keep allowing devastation to be our children's wake up call. There should be an alarm that goes off before disaster strikes. For many, the disaster ends up being their death. For others it's two or three decades in prison.

This was not the fate Harriet Tubman had in mind when she marched us from slavery to freedom. How her spirit must quake at the many that have been broken by poverty's brutal whip only to end up right back on a 21st century prison plantation. How the Martins, the Malcolms, the Medgars, and the mighty Mandelas of our history must agonize at our failings. Whose fault is it really when a child terrorizes his own neighborhood? Whose duty is it to stop him, heal him, and guide him back to the love of self? Is it ever his fault alone? As a living example of a very out of control and troubled youth that our culture seems to excel at creating, I do not pretend to have all the answers. But I do have a frontline view of the problems and I'm committed to doing the work to find solutions.

I can attest that no matter how convincing our masks appear to be, troubled young men like me do care. We lie (mostly to ourselves) when we behave as if we don't. Once I found myself all alone in this world I was forced to dig deep. I started to truly self-reflect and get to know myself in ways I never had. I realized that when I shut down to play a role, I had shut out the world which included the purest parts of myself. I was surprised by what I started to learn. I was much more than I once thought. I had been selling myself short with the labels I imposed on myself. I didn't even know that I was actually a handsome kid with a great sense of humor, and above average intellect. I was unconsciously insecure. I imagined that my criminal behaviors were the sum and substance of me. I had never looked in the mirror and seen what others did. In my mind I was an animal; I wasn't worth much at all, so I acted accordingly. Yes, I had been called handsome and been given reassuring compliments, but I never believed them to be genuine. I was my own worst enemy and toughest critic.

I kept digging, and I kept finding gold. Yes, I found some lumps of coal too; things I did not like and needed to address. But overall, I was learning that I was worthy. I was worthy of joy, a good life, redemption, a second chance; a lot more than I thought. The pennies I had chased after, destroyed lives for, shattered friendships over, and even the pain I used as an excuse to do all those things could never outweigh or diminish my value as a human being and a child of God. The more I found my true worth, the more remorse I felt for all my actions. Previously, I was only sorry I had been caught, now I was being forced to count the cost of my actions. I wanted to apologize to my victims, but for the most part, it would be impossible. Many of them were unknown to me. I had hurt so many with no real regard, I didn't keep a record. And there was no way I'd be able to speak to the deceased. Saying "Sorry" to the family felt wholly inadequate without something substantive or tangible to accompany mere words.

So, I took my heavy heart to God. I found that direction was attached to the sanctuary. There was simply no way I could ever change my past. There was also no way I could ignore it and live in some alternative reality. I had to take ownership of all its parts if I was ever to achieve the redemption I yearned for. In the midst of this struggle and these revelations I got a visit from a cold case detective. It was March 9, 2009. I had been incarcerated for fifteen years and I was being housed in Clinton Correctional Facility, a maximum-security prison in Dannemora, NY. He came to see me about an old unsolved homicide case. He was investigating the incident discussed in chapter twelve.

I always knew that someone would come eventually. I was glad to finally face it. I soon learned I would do so alone. Everyone involved blamed every single detail on me. I looked at each statement the detective had against me and knew I had left quite the impression. There were statements from people who knew me my entire life and each one had got it wrong, and I had to deal with it. I thought someone would say I was a troubled kid, or that there was a time when I had been full of life and love. But no one remembered Derrel, he'd been subsumed for far too long underneath a very convincing character commonly known as "Lil Dee." At first, I wanted to fight the case. I knew I was not the person I had been painted as and I was not the only person responsible for what went down that night. I refused to just accept the terms that were being offered to me. It's not that I wanted to fight what was; I was fighting for the person I was struggling to become.

Eventually a court order was issued to the state, and I was turned over to Erie County, in Buffalo New York. After fifteen years, I was back in the holding center where it all started when I was sixteen. The place smelled the same. It was enveloped in the stench of hopelessness, urine, feces, vomit, and blood. When I was given my identification bracelet it had my real name on it. Here I could be who my parents had named me, and I protested. I was Derrell Austin now. I didn't even know if most of my family and friends would know me by my real name. The guards refused to allow me to be held under an alias; so after all those years, I was forced to adjust again. This proved to be a problem for my family. They kept coming to visit me and being told there was no Derrell Austin in custody. My family thought I was giving them the wrong location of where I was being held. Then they concluded that I was losing my mind. It took days for all of us to realize Derrel Moore, the real me, had been resurrected. I had been so far removed from reality that even I didn't know my own name.

After months of fighting over what was, in order to protect what could be, my attorney and I had a long talk. He told me he could absolutely win the case. He wanted to fight it. I no longer did, and I told him so. I gave him several lame excuses about being tired of the county jail, the treatment, the food, and the inmates that were using unorthodox tactics, becoming jailhouse informants, and creating cases on innocent people. To his credit, he ignored all my excuses. He deemed them to be the nonsense they were. He said if you did it, you can plead guilty, if not we fight. I chose not to fight. I was tired and chose to take the plea. I took my time, and as the person I was starting to become, I did my best to apologize to the deceased's family for the person I had been. Those empty words meant nothing to them as I knew they would. I had nothing else this system could hold against me. At least nothing worth an ounce of the pain I had caused.

The time I was sentenced to seemed insignificant to the deceased's family. They had no idea the true price I had already paid for my past. I had been paying a King's ransom for many years. I knew from talks with my conscience that I would be paying for the rest of my life. I left the holding center knowing I had no more outstanding debts to pay, nothing else held over my head, no more shoes waiting to drop. That would be my last time in criminal court. I also knew it wasn't the highest court. I would still be judged some day in my entirety by God. Knowing this, I took the long ride back to prison consumed with thoughts of that day. I started to think in terms of legacy. How could I transition from my poor start to my impressive finish? I wanted to be able to make the case to The Most High that when I knew better, I actually did better. Although I could not do it over, I wanted Him to see that when I could, I did different.

I had to figure out how to stay out my own way. This would prove difficult in a cage where great thoughts came attached to heart wrenching regret, and chains. The more I healed, the greater my ideals became. The cell closed in around me as my regret grew thick. Now I knew what was meant by "ignorance is bliss." As I grew, my frustration ran the risk of boiling over into bitterness. As I built myself up, putting myself back together one piece at a time, I could not help but wonder "what if?" What if things had been different?

What if I hadn't left the house that night? What if I never moved back to Buffalo? What if I had told someone the truth when I was six?

I would pray, asking that my Lord would listen. I'd sometimes whisper "why me?" in my prayers. My experience has taught me that you don't need to be a religious person to receive revelation for your life. I am sure everyone has had what we call "light bulb moments." Mine was the answer to that whisper, "why me?" It wasn't just my desire to change that made the difference; even a fool will desire change when they hit rock bottom. It was the answer to my whisper that would be the catalyst for all my efforts, for all the days of my life.

We are born to struggle. Our life is designed for it. So "why me?" is a question asked from a place of self-doubt. It comes from our insecurity. God placed a path before me that he knew no one else could handle if chosen. For years I had mishandled that which God gifted me. Instead, I made excuses. I played the victim of circumstances. This cost me a great deal, but it didn't have to keep costing me. The answer to my whisper eventually grew louder than the question. *"Why not you?"* Was I too good to struggle, or too weak? Better question, did I feel unworthy of God's attention and the duty attached? I had to face these questions and stop asking why. This was my reality. It was not going to change simply because I decided to change. If anything, it only grew worse because when I was unconscious, I was also unaware of the huge responsibility resting on me. Now I understood what was required of me. Change started to seem like a job, and it was. The hours were long, the work went without much praise. There were no days off. The upside was that I knew it would eventually pay off.

The way I started to feel, the confidence I developed; it was great. I used to be unable to look most people in the eyes. I fumbled with words and felt uncertain of every aspect of my life. I had been an insecure and broken person living from a foundation of fear. There is no worse prison than the ones people build for themselves out of fear of being hurt. In the middle of a maximum-security prison, doing a life sentence is where I was able to find my freedom. I had been running from shadows hiding in the shade. I had been searching high and low for liberation when all along I held the key. It's like when you are in a rush to go to work feverishly searching for the car keys, only to realize the whole time they were in your hand.

CHAPTER SEVENTEEN
Thank God I Survived Being Lil Dee

With all the guns sprayed at me with sincere effort to end my young life, I can only thank God that I survived. These overt and obvious attempts were not the only threats to my fragile life and the more subtle attempts on my life were no less deadly. As a boy those things I was exposed to must not be ignored. To disturb, and tamper with the psychological make-up of a child is to run the risk of completely ruining that child. Keeping this in mind, we must do better with how we love and shield our babies from the evils of this world. From knee high I was under attack from every angle. My brain was mush, and almost immediately being fashioned to fail. My brain cells were corrupted, and my behaviors programmed. Then I was unleashed on the world and expected to be fully formed, well adjusted, and responsible for my actions.

The overabundance of violence, sex, and hustling

213

I observed as a child showed up in the young man I became. One area where the ills of my environment showed up and showed out was in my promiscuity. My sexual activities from a young age were on the level of rock star status. I had sexual encounters with women whose name I did not know. It didn't matter where we were. I would have sex in any place imaginable. The riskier it was, the more interested I would be. It was never about the sex itself; it was about how the sex subdued my pain, disguised my insecurities, and pacified my fears. Sex was my security blanket. Where others would chain smoke to sooth themselves, I abused my body, and it put me at risk. I was having an insane amount of meaningless sex with random women who were adults, and girls my age; and I wasn't using any protection. There were days when I would have sex with three or four different grown women or girls with no regard for safety. I didn't think about the dangers this posed, and I didn't care. I never once stopped to consider the consequences at all. I cannot recall one day when I ever felt like what I was doing was wrong. Where I'm from, it was normal.

One day a girl about my age at the time approached me while I was standing on a friend's porch. We were about fourteen at the time. She did not ask me my name; she didn't even say hello. Her only words to me were, "do you want to fuck?" I immediately said, "Yes," and took her in the house where we had sex.

We shared no words, it was not special, and when it was over, she left just as quickly as she came. I know now that I should have been shocked by her words. I should have refused. But back then I didn't have the ability to be shocked or feel it was wrong. I never saw her again, I didn't know her name, and I do not know her story, but I'd bet my life that hers was just as complicated as my own. I think our hurt souls called out to one another and connected. In the streets they say, "Game recognize game," but another saying that is just as true is "trauma recognize trauma," and she recognized me. Our shared hurt and desperation allowed us to communicate without words.

I don't recount this story to romanticize disfunction, but to highlight how abnormal a child's behaviors can become when exposed to all sorts of trauma. I now know that we were two acutely troubled teens, going unnoticed, and unnurtured in the proper way. We were trying to regain control and replace the memories of all the horrors in our heads. I can only pray for her and hope that she found a way to heal. I think back on all my reckless behaviors, specifically the sexual ones, and wonder. What if there are children out there that I never got a chance to know. I cringe at the thought of children being out there that I conceived, who never got to know their father. In my experience there is always a price to pay for reckless behavior. Thankfully, I am healthy and did not contract any diseases. There is no other explanation for this other than God's unearned grace and limitless mercy.

Speaking of mercy, as I stated above, I've been in situations where bullets flew past my head more than once. I've seen the actual fire burst and smoke rise from that missile up close as someone tried to kill me. I still have the scar from one instance where a bullet grazed my head in pursuit of my life. These were warnings, and each one presented me with the opportunity to change course. But these events never caused me to think twice. To the contrary, they did the exact opposite. As a teenager who had looked death in the face more than once and lived to tell the tale, I felt invincible. These near-death experiences inspired me to raise the level of my delinquent behavior.

In one of these instances a car pulled up on me as I was about to cross the street. A machine gun styled weapon; the kind only meant for use in world wars was pushed out the window. The gunman had it inches from my stomach and squeezed the trigger with the intent of cutting me in half. I stood frozen, thinking, "I knew it would end this way. I don't care." Then the gun's firing pen clicked as it hit metal. The gunman had failed to chamber the weapon with a bullet. I quickly retreated through the yard as the gunman corrected his error. He was soon sending a barrage of bullets from his automatic weapon in hot pursuit of my one-hundred-and-fifty-pound body. He missed and now my plan was to respond in a way he would not live to regret.

A person with any sense would have reflected on how close they had come to death, but I had no sense. With every escape I became more arrogant, I believed myself to be unstoppable. I got my own weapon of choice, and my first stop was the gunman's mother's house. I had eaten at this home, even slept there, now I had gone to cause carnage. Thank God she was outside when I pulled up. His mother was a sweet and precious lady. I greeted her as she was getting out of her car and asked where her sons were. After she explained they weren't there, I asked her to tell them that I came by, and then left without incident. The sight of her had appealed to whatever humanity I had left. But Lil Dee was still lurking in the background.

After Derrel granted clemency to the gunman's mother, Lil Dee went directly to his baby's mother's house to complete the mission. The gunman used to be my friend, so I knew where his family members lived and had been to their homes. The baby was an infant, but Lil Dee had no moral compass. Someone had just tried to kill him...again so he was in survival mode, which left no room for any regard for life. Lil Dee wanted the gunman to feel what he wouldn't, which was fear.

At the time I thought I was (and pretended to

be) fearless. But decades removed from that night and from that person, hindsight tells me that fear is actually what was driving me. I thought the remedy was to instill fear in everyone that threatened my existence. They needed to embrace this fear because I refused to. When we got to the house where the gunman's daughter lived my comrade at the time Monet tried to encourage me to wait since the gunman's car wasn't there. But my plan was to leave a message of my presence where his heart lived. At that point I was beyond reason. Then God intervened again, providing me with a way back from the brink. When I got out of the cab that we used for things like this I instructed the driver to keep going up the street, then turn around to pick me up.

Then I saw her. The posture of my heart shifted as I saw the mother and innocent child on the porch. What happened next has been understood and interpreted and retold from many different perspectives, but here's the truth. I waited for the mother and child to enter the front door. As she closed the front door, I ran onto the porch. I was familiar with the house. I knew its layout. I knew that it was a duplex two-family home and that she'd have to walk down a hallway and then open a second door to get inside her apartment. So, as she walked down the hallway to her apartment, I purposely shot into the living room while she and the baby were out of the line of fire. I was a pretty good shot back then. I had taken shooting lessons with friends when I lived in Bradford, PA, and we often played a shooting game called "pitching quarters" where we'd try to shoot quarters that had been pitched into ditches in the woods. I was confident that I had the skills to get my point across without causing them harm. I wanted everyone, especially the men that tried to kill me to think that they just got lucky; or that it was a miracle that the bullets missed them. I wanted everyone to see me as a madman, and they did (at the time, maybe I was).

Ironically, in my mind, I believed I had done right by the mother and child. I honestly viewed what I had done as a noble deed, which illustrates just how sick and twisted my reality was. These are some examples of how I played with death and danced with insanity in my teen years. I could spend days talking about the many events not listed here, many of which could have led to my death. Instead, I would much rather acknowledge God's grace for sparing my life as I lived so recklessly and at times behaved so cruelly. God's presence existed in ways I did not recognize and did not have the capacity to appreciate. As a teen, there was no way I could imagine that there was a purpose connected to my improbable escapes.

The presence of God was even more evident during my incarceration. He had lovingly guided my life's events in such a way that I could eventually rise above all the bad I had done. I came to state prison angry, filled with frustration, and ready to continue living out my pain. In many ways I actually did get lost in this pain, but it was always controlled by something bigger than me. While incarcerated I never acted violently or intentionally hurt people the way I had previously done. Instead, I involved myself with certain activities in prison that had the potential to lead to violent behavior. I often dealt drugs and made large sums of money in the prison system, which often leads to violence, and new criminal charges. I would always come extremely close to getting caught by staff or seriously injured by envious prisoners. But just like on the streets, I always escaped serious harm, so I continued to believe I was special. I thought I was untouchable due to my own genius. In truth, there has always been a presence bigger than me overshadowing my life, allowing me to take my knocks and make my mistakes, while protecting me and patiently waiting for me to turn to Him.

I've taken more knocks than I can count and I'm sure I'm not done yet (as long as we're alive we never are). However, I'm no longer that unaware, apathetic, and callous kid. I've dismembered my mask. I no longer take chances with my life because now I know its value. While I continue to examine my past and try to understand how I became Lil Dee,

I've stopped making excuses for my actions. I know what was my fault and what wasn't. I've forgiven all my victimizers and most importantly I've forgiven myself for having lived my life as a victim. I still find myself incarcerated, and I don't know when or if I will ever be released. I am working on it, and praying I will achieve it so I can fulfill my purpose.

One of the wonderful things about God is that he wastes nothing. The seemingly wasted parts of my life are exactly what qualifies me to help repair the hearts and the minds of the most troubled youth among us. Because of my lived experience I am fluent in the language of the hard knock life, and the truth is few who work with delinquent teens are; not really. My Ph.D. from the School of Hard Knocks will grant me entrance to the hearts and minds of troubled youth in a way that a Harvard degree never could.

This is how I will pay my debt to the society that I've caused so much harm. This is my mission, and I have been called and equipped to accomplish it. My restitution will not consist of mere words. I will continue to do the work. Today, as I write these final words from a cage I have a smile on my face, and joy in my heart, knowing that the work has already begun. I know that several young men that looked up to me in here are now back out there with you, and based in part on my mentorship, they've been able overcome their "Lil Dee".

I've lived a life of turmoil; I was reckless on every level. I've been tested in many ways, including some that great people of history have endured, and I too survived. I thank God that I stand bloodied, but unbowed, tested without failure, battered yet unbroken, pushed to the limits but still living. I can truly say that I am not weary, I am willing. And I am grateful that I survived being Lil Dee.

CONCLUSION

I made this book as short as possible and left out as much as I could. I must stress that this book is not intended to in any way glorify my poor behavior. It wasn't even written to highlight my troubled childhood. Its primary purpose is not to profit off my storied past. I did this to expose some of the complex realities in our impoverished communities in America. Anyone watching the news can see that there are "Lil Dee's" in every community. We come in every color. We are male and female. We live in cities and the suburbs, and we need help. I offer just a glimpse into the mindset of our children who eventually become those that are filling our cemeteries and prisons. This alarming reality will not resolve itself, nor is the answer more prisons to house the predictable results of society's failings.

As a product of this environment, I caused pain to many innocent people. If you conclude that I (and those like me in your community) have no redeemable qualities, consider those hurt by me, and those that will be hurt by others like me. This is not a Black or Brown issue alone. This is an issue that the world and all of us as a whole must address. The materials that mix together to make a troubled child like me are not isolated to the streets of Buffalo. This mixture is readily available in every community in our country. This is a problem that is pervasive in our culture.

At the age of fourteen I was crossing state lines alone taking my self-hate to places unprepared to deal with my madness. As we become increasingly connected via travel and the internet, it is less likely that society's inconvenient problems can be segregated and contained in specific areas. Don't be fooled. There are "Lil Dee's" in privileged communities too. Although the "D" may stand for Dylan instead of Derrick or Dyquan, the pain and disillusionment that expresses itself in senseless violence is the same.

And it's not just America, "Lil Dee" is international. I recently read a very heart wrenching book about the plight of children in South Asia. The story was chilling and made me want to pledge the thirty-five dollars per month it asked for to help one child. I am still trying to fit it in my budget if I can get a prison program that will pay me that much per month. As I continued to read the many stories of rape and brutality, I could not help but notice the similarities. Their experiences in South Asia almost mirror the kids in impoverished communities of America. The only difference being that there is no organization in existence tackling the problem internationally. I find it troubling and telling that we live in the world's leading nation for humanitarian work, helping people all over the globe but no one ever came to save me from me. I know there are local organizations struggling to do as much as possible. I commend them for their efforts and their compassion. This work should not be ignored, and while programs do exist, they are just a small portion of what is necessary to seriously address this challenge.

The criminal justice system is filled with children stuck in a condition they were born to, not one they created. There are two states, New York, and North Carolina prosecuting children as adults. The entire country has no system in place to see how our youth have become so out of control. People are being trained to prosecute our children, while others are being trained to receive our children in the prison system. There is no one being trained to redirect, nurture, and rehabilitate our children. I have been one of these subjects. Over two decades in prison, and there has not been one moment of one day that even one person has come to try and figure out how, and why I ended up here.

There was only a judicial system void of justice that put labels on me that I could not spell and didn't understand. Then I was placed in a system where you are required to become even worse to survive or become even more of a victim. It almost sets up an impossible choice guaranteeing you two options; become a career criminal, or a lifetime victim. So where do we start? Do we simply acknowledge the errors? Do better with our future children and forget those of yesterday? What happens to the hearts and minds of those we have failed? What happened to those that contributed to their failure? To you, those of you like me, with my spirit, and with similar pain, you must also do the work. You cannot continue to hurt as you pretend it's all good. As you talk, walk, and act in ignorance I know you secretly hate it, but it's become a method of survival. It is time to destroy this mindset, demolish your mask, and demand your humanity.

The first person you must demand it from is yourself. You must seek your liberation from the falsehoods you created in order to allow yourself to live in deviance. You are worth a billion times more than what you have bartered your soul for. I know how eloquently you spoke to your spirit and convinced yourself of what "they" did or did not do. How "they" designed it all this way just to stick it to you. I am not here to point fingers; we have all played our roles. My prayer is that you stop focusing on what *they* did or did not do long enough to reflect on you.

They may never come, *they* may never help, and *they* may never change. Whoever *they* may be to you, it is time that you be more of a friend to yourself than *they* have been, or ever will be. Please do better for yourself; liberate yourself from the chains **you** have wrapped around yourself and become so comfortable carrying.

Appeal to your own humanity and if they never try to do right by you, it won't matter one bit, because you will have done enough for yourself. Moms, dads, uncles, aunts, siblings, friends, and more, I do apologize. I simply do not have all the answers, in truth no one does. I pray you will love on your troubled children harder, and fight for their liberation from the pain that inspires their madness. Do not give up on them no matter how easy they make it, because even rodents have some redeemable qualities. If you open your heart and mind and give it the effort, surely you can find a few in your fellow man (even those of us that have behaved as beasts).

I have done as best as I could with my current hand, and I promise as a redeemed soul, I will continue to pay back my debts to my fellow man. Many will decide I am just an animal that deserves all I've gotten. You have every right to your opinion, and your feelings. I can only suggest that if you dare to judge, be daring enough to save. Take your judgment to the troubled children in communities across our nation and appeal to the hearts of the lost with compassion and a helping hand.

In our society we should never conclude that a child cannot change. A child whose brain has yet to fully develop should never be sentenced to life in prison. This speaks more to our shortcomings (and perhaps our own inhumanity) as a society than it does the actions of a child. We must do better, and the first step is to demand a better system of prevention, reform and rehabilitation for our children.

*****Since the original writing of the manuscript for this book, the author went to the parole board for the third time, and after twenty-two years was released. So be on the lookout for what he does next.

The story of my life after prison bars is ***COMING SOON!***

Sign up for the OMP newsletter to get updates on the release of Book 2

pages.onemoorepage.com/email_list_landing_page

ABOUT THE AUTHOR

Derrel Moore Jr. is a Buffalo native who grew up in the New York State prison system. He is a published author, a mentor, and a community activist who focuses on serving troubled youth and assisting ex-convicts with successful re-entry into society. Additionally, Derrel is a speaker and frequent panelist on topics including criminal justice reform, juvenile delinquency, violence prevention, and prison reform from the perspective of the accused and convicted. Derrel is a proud father, grandfather, son and husband who places his faith in the Most Merciful, the Highest, the One True God.

Learn More About Derrel Moore Jr.

www.onemoorepage.com

Subscribe to the Confessions of the Accused YouTube Channel

https://www.youtube.com/@confessionsoftheaccused

Follow on Instagram

https://www.instagram.com/confessionsoftheaccused

Follow on Instagram

https://www.facebook.com/confessionsoftheaccused

Get the OMP newsletter for updates on new books and upcoming events

pages.onemoorepage.com/email_list_landing_page

Learn More About the COTA Community and Mentorship opportinities

pages.onemoorepage.com/cota

CONFESSIONS OF THE ACCUSED

CONFESSIONS OF THE ACCUSED

Made in the USA
Monee, IL
17 July 2023

39408217R00152